China and the West

CHINA AND THE WEST

Wolfgang Franke

Translated by

R. A. WILSON

UNIVERSITY OF SOUTH CAROLINA PRESS

COLUMBIA

Contents

Preface

This book does not pretend to be a history, or even a summary, of the relations between China and the West. Rather, it represents an attempt to describe the historical development of a number of problems which are characteristic of China's relations with the West, and which still have a decisive influence thereon at the present time. Thus the political, economic and military background of the encounter between China and the West is only referred to when it is necessary to the understanding of the questions with which we are dealing. In this context, facts which are easily accessible elsewhere are less important than the objective knowledge and subjective ideas which people in China and the West had of each other. For it was these on which their attitude to each other was mainly based, and which even today are of decisive importance in their relationship with each other. We have actually discussed the Chinese view of the West in greater detail than Western ideas about China. For this reason, the book is entitled *China and the West* and not *The West and China*. The author's first concern has been to help the reader to understand the Chinese point of view and the Chinese attitude towards the West. It is true that the Chinese attitude is to a large degree a reaction to the behaviour of the West, so that the latter must be taken into account, and will frequently be criticised. In general, however, it is not the intention of the author to judge or to condemn, but to show the heavy burden of mistakes and misunderstandings, some of them going back several centuries, with which the relationship between China and the West is weighed down, in the hope that he may perhaps do a little towards removing this burden.

The connections between China and Russia, which is itself a part of the West, are only occasionally touched upon. Russia is the only Western country which shares a long land frontier with China. Thus the relationship of China to Russia is unique, and can only be equated to a limited degree with her relationship with other Western countries. Even at the present time China's relationship to the Soviet Union presents a series of special problems which are far from being identical with those discussed in the present volume. Consequently, China's relationship with Russia is not discussed.

Since this book is intended more for the general reader who is interested in the subject, rather than for specialists, no reference to sources is given except for direct quotations. The literature used in each section is given in a bibliography at the end of the book. In a few cases the author has incorporated into the text passages from more detailed studies which he has published elsewhere, especially from the article 'Zur anti-imperialistischen Bewegung in China' ('On the Anti-Imperialist Movement in China'), in *Saeculum* 5, 1954, pp. 337–358. Other works of his own of which use has been made are given in the bibliography. If the notes on passages translated in the text only refer to the Chinese source, the author has made the translation himself; if there is also a reference to another work, the translation given there has been consulted. If no Chinese source is given, then the passage quoted is based exclusively on the translation mentioned.

Apart from literary sources, the author has made use, especially in the later chapters, of his own experiences during a thirteen-year stay in China from 1937 to 1950. Mme Chün-Yin Franke Hu has also put forward the Chinese point of view in many discussions on the present subject, in the course of which she has brought to light a number of problems, and has therefore made an essential contribution to the composition of this book. Dr. Barbara Krafft and Dr. Bernhard Grossmann have kindly read through the whole manuscript and made a number of valuable suggestions. The author, of course, accepts sole responsibility for the entire text.

In the transcription of Chinese names, titles and expressions the Giles-Wade system, which is most widely used throughout the world, has been used. Names in general currency are given in their familiar form.

On the way to East Asia in the Indian Ocean, March 1962.

I

China and the West before the 13th Century

Before the 13th century, that is, before the Mongols founded an empire extending over both Europe and Asia, the different parts of the huge Eurasian land mass scarcely knew any more about each other than did the continents which were separated by the ocean before the great discoveries made by the Spanish and Portuguese. In particular, the regions which lay at the furthest extremes of the continent, and in which the highest civilisations developed—Southern and Western Europe on the one hand, and China on the other—remained entirely or virtually unknown to each other for centuries.

In the classical age of ancient Greece and Rome practically nothing was known of China. The names Seres and Sera first occur from time to time at the end of the pre-Christian era, under the Emperor Augustus; they signify the Silk-people and the Land of Silk. In ancient Rome, silk was very expensive and much sought after. All that was known was that it came from the distant East. Thus the word for silk was simply used for the remote and unknown people who produced it, and did not carry any implication as to their exact position or ethnic status. At the beginning of our era we find, in addition to Sera and Seres, and without reference to them, names such as Sinae, called Thinai in Greek, which are used by the authors of the *Periplus Maris Rubri*, by Pliny the Elder (1st century A.D.), in Ptolemy (2nd century A.D.), in Marinos of Tyre (2nd century A.D.) and in many other Greek and Roman geographers of that period.

Nothing was known apart from the names, however, and no one had any idea what they might possibly refer to. All that was known was that was where silk came from. It was not known how silk was made. Thus many fantastic legends were repeated about the production of silk and the Silk-people.

Some, for example, told of the savage and inhospitable nation of the Seres, who lived at the end of the world. No more firmly based information was available and fantasy went unchecked. And the thought of that time could not conceive in any case how anything that lay outside the Roman Empire could be other than savage and uncivilised!

Numerous suggestions have been put forward as to the origin of the name Seres, but none has been generally accepted. The most likely seems to be that which derives it from the Chinese word for silk, pronounced at the present day *szu*, which probably ended in its earlier form with a velar consonant. But even this derivation is extremely problematic.

More is known about the origin of the name Sina, from which comes the modern name China. In the 3rd Century B.C. there existed in the North-West of China, where the routes to Central and Western Asia begin, a powerful state called Ch'in, which in 246 B.C. brought all China under its control. The royal family of Ch'in then ruled China as the Ch'in Dynasty. The inhabitants of that state in the North-West, and later the people of the whole of China, called themselves, *Ch'in-jen*, 'the people of Ch'in'. The name was carried to India by China's Central Asian neighbours as *Cina, Maha-Cina*. Its origin was not recognised by the later Chinese translators of Indian Buddhist writings, and they transcribed it into Chinese as *Chih-na*. This became Shina in Japanese, which up to the end of the second World War was the regular name for China in that language. It is still used in Japan at the present day. Probably before the beginning of the Christian era, the name *Cina* travelled from India through Asia Minor, Greece and into the Roman Empire. This derivation of the name China has not been disputed seriously in recent years and can be regarded as generally accepted.

A few centuries later, somewhat more substantial information concerning China reached the West in association with a third name. About 630 A.D. the Byzantine chronicler Theophylactos of Simocatta described a country called Taugast and its rulers. According to him, the people of this country venerated images of the gods, had just laws and displayed a calm and unhurried judgement. He also described courtly customs and details about a war, all of which correspond to historical events and institutions which are known from the Chinese sources. It has been generally recognised for more than fifty years that the information given by Theophylactos can only refer to China, and that he must have obtained it from Central Asian Turks. The only disagreement concerns the origin of the name Taugast. But the view is now widely held that Taugast is derived from the name of the Tungus royal family of Toba (Wei) who ruled in North China in the 6th century. The original pronunciation of the name could perhaps have been *T'ak-pat*, and is known in Turkish as *Taybac*. Although Theophylactos has little to tell about Taugast, he provides the most accurate information about China which was available to the West before the 13th century. Of course it was not realised that Taugast, Seres and Sinae basically referred to the same country or people in the Far East.

Not much more was known by the Chinese about the West during the same period. Here again, legend held sway. One story purported to tell of the journey into the farthest West carried out by King Mu of the Chou dynasty at the beginning of the first millenium B.C., to visit the legendary *Hsi-wang-mu*, the 'Queen Mother of the West', about whom many fantastic stories were told. In the 19th century, and even at the beginning of the 20th century, the attempt was made to identify the *Hsi-Wang-Mu* with the Arabian Queen of Sheba, mentioned in the Bible (1 Kings 10) as an ally of King Solomon—this, of course, is an untenable hypothesis. But as early as the end of the 2nd century B.C. more accurate information about the Far West reached China. For the first time, a Chinese embassy, known by the name of its leader Chang Ch'ien, penetrated into Western Central Asia as far as the region of the Upper Oxus (Amu-Darja). There it came into contact with outposts of Greek and Roman civilisation, and received from them the firm impression that there existed another highly developed civilisation outside of China. Apart from what they saw and experienced themselves, they heard a great deal more about the countries which lay far to the West and their civilisation. The account of their journey, which has come down to us, is an extraordinarily interesting document. It was laid before the Emperor, and at that time, as later, must have had a considerable effect. Of course even the news of a well-organised state and law-abiding nations in the Far West was not able seriously to disturb the already fixed view of the world which placed China in the centre of the universe. Then as later, China regarded herself as the centre and the sole source of all culture and civilisation, with the Chinese Emperor at the heart of everything, as universal ruler, and the uncivilised barbarian nations round about. Yet the importance of the embassy of Chang Ch'ien cannot be overestimated. It brought into being a constant association between China and Central and Western Asia which from then on was only rarely interrupted. By way of this association, elements of Chinese civilisation reached the West, and Chinese civilisation was much stimulated and enriched from Central Asia.

From the beginning of the Christian era onwards, the name which was particularly used of the West in China was that of Ta Ch'in. There was, however, no clear picture of the location of this country. In the year 97 A.D. a Chinese ambassador crossed Central Asia and reached the Persian Gulf. In the 'Official History' of that period, the *Han shu*, we read:

> He reached T'iao-chih (probably on the east coast of the Persian Gulf) and passed through An-hsi (the Persian part of Parthia) to the shore of the Western Sea, from where Ta Ch'in could be seen.[1]

Besides Ta Ch'in, the name Li-kan appeared, and in the 6th or 7th century A.D., also the name Fu-lin. The three names, and what they stood for, were not clearly distinguished from one another; they are all evidently used to refer to the great

[1] *Ch'ien Han shu*, ed. Wu chou t'ung-wen, ch. 118, 21 b.

unknown empire in the West, that is, therefore, the eastern parts of the Roman Empire. The origin of the three names themselves has been much disputed by modern scholars. Numerous hypotheses have been skilfully and obstinately defended. There is agreement only that the name Fu-lin is derived from Rome, that is, from its Iranian and Persian form From. It has been suggested that Ta Ch'in and Li-kan might be identified with Ctesiphon and Seleukia, the great double city on the Tigris. But this is only one of many hypotheses, none of which has been generally accepted. Even though much that is fantastic and legendary is recorded in Chinese sources concerning the Far West, it was known nevertheless that a great, well-ordered and civilised empire existed there.

In general it is clear that before the foundation of the Mongol Empire, Western Europe and China had some idea of each other's existence, but knew next to nothing concrete. A large part was played by fantasy and fable, even though the Chinese accounts contain a few more definite facts than those of the West. Neither the Greeks and Romans nor the Chinese looked beyond the countries which bordered directly on their own civilisation. Both saw themselves as the centre and source of all civilisation and culture.

In spite of this very slight direct knowledge of each other, in this early period of the relationship between China and the West, not a few elements of Western civilisation found their way to the East and *vice versa*. For example, in the 6th century hellenistic elements found their way through India and Central Asia into Chinese art in the form of what is known as the Gandhara style. Up to the 15th century, China was far ahead not only of the West, but also of most oriental civilisations, in the sphere of natural science and technology. Thus the inventions which found their way from China to the West in the course of the centuries were very much more numerous and important than those which travelled in the reverse direction. For example, the West received from China the wheelbarrow, the sailing carriage, the cross-bow, the iron-chain suspension-bridge, the magnetic compass and its use for navigation, paper, printing, and movable-type printing, the kite, porcelain and much else.

II

The First Direct Link between China and Europe during the Mongol Period

1. GIOVANNI DE PIANO CARPINI

From the 7th and 8th centuries on, there was a lively maritime trade between Persia and Arabia, and China. Right up to the 13th century the Persians and Arabs had factories and trading depots in the Chinese ports of Ch'üanchou (Fukien) and Chiangtu (the later Yangchou in South Kiangsu). But it is not known whether the Persians or Arabs carried accounts of China to Western Europe.

It was the foundation of the Mongol Empire by Ghengiz Khan in the 13th century which first made possible a direct link between Western Europe and Eastern Asia. The empire of Genghiz Khan extended from the Ukraine in the West to the borders of China in the East. After his death, the Mongols finally succeeded in bringing all China under their rule, so that in 1279 it became part of the Mongol Empire.

In 1245 Pope Innocent IV sent the Italian Franciscan Giovanni de Piano Carpini with an official letter to the court of the Mongol Khan. In this letter the Pope demanded that the Khan should cease his attacks against other nations, especially against Christian nations, and that he should become a Christian himself. The knowledge that there were Nestorian Christians amongst the Mongols may have given rise to this extremely Utopian expectation. Piano Carpini, with a few companions, travelled through Southern Russia and Central Asia, and in the summer of 1246 arrived at the Khan's capital in Mongolia, west of Karakorum. He remained there more than three months, and returning by approximately the same route, arrived home in the summer of the following year.

Piano Carpini has left a rather brief account of his journey, which contains in particular interesting geographical, historical and ethnological details about the Mongol Empire and its peoples. He only mentions China incidentally, giving it the name Kitai. This short passage was the first trustworthy account of China which had reached Western Europe. It reads as follows:

> The people of Kitai are heathens and have their own way of writing. It is said that they possess the Old and the New Testaments, and accounts of the lives of the Fathers, and have hermits and buildings which are similar to our churches, and in which they pray at fixed times. They say that they also have a number of saints like ours. They pray only to one God, and honour our Lord Jesus Christ and believe in an eternal life. On the other hand, baptism is completely unknown amongst them. They honour and esteem our Holy Scriptures, regard Christians favourably, and carry out very many works of mercy; in short, they seem to be very kind and benevolent people. They have no beards and their faces are very similar to those of the Mongols, except that they are not so wide. They speak a remarkable language of their own, and are the cleverest experts in the world in all the inventions of human ingenuity. Their country is very rich in cereals, wine, gold, silver, silk and everything that human nature needs for its sustenance.[1]

Elsewhere, Piano Carpini names in addition to Kitai the kingdom of Mangia, with which the Mongols were at war. From then on, China was known in the west as Kitai or Cathay, and even at the present day the name for China in Russian and other East European languages is Kitai or something similar. Its origin is the name of the Kitan, a people frequently known as the Tungus, who ruled over North China from 916 to 1124, with the Chinese dynastic name Liao. After they were driven from North China by another steppe people, the Juchen of the Chin dynasty, those of the Kitan who survived set up a new kingdom in Turkestan in the basin of the river Syr-darja (Yaxartes), the centre of which lay north of the present day

---

[1] F. Risch, *Johann de Piano Carpini. Geschichte der Mongolen und Reisebericht 1245-1247.* Leipzig 1930, pp. 119-120.

Tashkent. It existed until 1218 under the name of Western Liao or Khara Kitai, that is 'Black Kitai'. The name of this non-Chinese tribe was applied by the Mongols and the other neighbouring nations in the first place only to Northern China, but later to the whole of China, as had earlier been the case with the names China and Taugast. The identity of Kitai and Sina was not recognised until the beginning of the 17th century.

The other name, Mangia or Manzi, was used by the Mongols for Southern China under the native Sung dynasty even after the Mongol conquest. *Man-tzu*—this is the origin of the name —is in fact the Chinese term for the non-Chinese aboriginal tribes in South and South West China. It contains a strong implication of contempt, and it was a great humiliation to the Chinese that the Mongols should use it on them. But the name Manzi did not remain long in use. Kitai or Cathay became the term used for the whole of China.

2. WILLIAM OF RUBRUK

A few years after the return of Piano Carpini another Franciscan, the Fleming William of Rubruk (Ruysbroeck) set out for the Far East. He had probably spoken to Piano Carpini after the latter's return, and had already heard a great deal about the Mongols during his own participation in the Crusades, and especially about the Nestorian Christian congregations there, and the favourable attitude of the Khan towards Christians. He planned, therefore, to undertake a journey to the capital of the Mongol Khan, and received the support of King Louis IX of France. Both the king and the Pope gave Rubruk letters to the Khan. The purpose of the enterprise was to make contact with the Mongols, in order eventually to make an alliance with them in the conflict with the Mohammedans for the liberation of the Holy Land. In May 1253 Rubruk set off from Constantinople and, crossing the Black Sea and the Crimea, travelled eastwards through Southern Russia and Central Asia to Karakorum. He remained there from April to August 1254 and then travelled back by the same route which

B

he had taken on his outward journey. The account he has left of his journey is much fuller than that of Piano Carpini. For Rubruk had made careful preparations for this journey, and one of his main intentions was to find out about the countries of the East. It is true that he did not reach China proper, and consequently China is only mentioned incidentally in his account. At the same time, he was the first to recognise that Kitai and Sera must be the same country, and he was also the first to notice the distinctive features of Chinese writing. This is what Rubruk writes concerning Kitai:

Beyond (to the east) lies great Cataia, the inhabitants of which, I believe, were known long ago as the Seres. From them are obtained the best silk goods, which were called 'serica' after the name of this people. The people themselves took the name Seres from one of their cities. I learnt from a reliable source that in that country there is a city with walls of silver and ramparts of gold. In this country there are many provinces, several of which have not yet been conquered by the Mongols. The sea stretches between them and India.

The inhabitants of Catai are small in stature and breathe strongly through the nose when they speak. In common with all orientals they have very narrow eyes. They are accomplished experts in every art and craft, and their doctors have an accurate knowledge of the healing powers of herbs and are well acquainted with the art of determining the condition of a sick man from his pulse. But they make no urinary tests, and know nothing about the urine. I have observed this, for many of them lived in Karakorum. And from long ago it has been their custom that every son must follow the calling of his father. . . .[1]

From the place where I met Mangu to Catai, it was twenty days' journey to the south-east. . . .[2]

Catai lies on the ocean, . . .[3]

The ordinary money of Catai is a piece of cotton cloth, as long and as wide as a hand, on which lines of writing are impressed and also the seal of Mangu. The inhabitants of Catai write with a brush such as painters use, and they include in a single character several letters, forming a word. . .[4]

[1] F. Risch, *Wilhelm von Rubruk. Reise zu den Mongolen 1253–1255*, Leipzig 1934, pp. 169–172.
[2] ibid. p. 223.   [3] ibid. p. 228.   [4] ibid. pp. 230–231.

3. MARCO POLO (1254–1324)

The true discoverer of China for the West was Marco Polo. He was born in 1254 into a Venetian merchant family. His father Nicolo and his brother Maffeo had been to the court of the Mongol Khan Khubilai in order to trade, and had set up a regular trading association between the Far East and Venice. As ambassadors of the Khan they had returned home with a letter to the Pope. In 1271 they left Italy again with the Pope's answer and took with them Marco, who was then seventeen years old. They travelled across the Mediterranean towards Central Asia and then by land through Mesopotamia to the Persian Gulf, by ship to Hormuz, and then northwards by land once again through Iran to the upper Oxus (Amu-darja), over the Pamir to Kashgar, and on through Khotan, Lop Nor, Kansu, North Shensi and Inner Mongolia. This was a different route from that taken previously by Piano Carpini and Rubruk. In 1275 the Polos arrived in Khubilai's summer capital Shangtu (north of Peking in Inner Mongolia).

The young Marco Polo possessed many talents and displayed a skilful, quick and reliable understanding as he journeyed through foreign countries and cities. He is said to have learned in a short time to speak not only Mongolian and Chinese, but also Uighur, Hsihsia (the Tangut language) and Tibetan. In this way he drew the attention of the Khan to himself and soon enjoyed his special favour. On numerous occasions the Khan sent Marco Polo as his official and ambassador into various parts of the Mongol Empire, and after the final overthrow of the Sung kingdom in the year 1279, he also sent him to China. Thus Marco Polo travelled from the capital Khanbalik (corresponding to present-day Peking) through Shansi, Shensi, Szuchuan, and Yünnan to Burma. In the course of this journey he also came in contact with Tibetans and collected information concerning Tibet. He went on another journey through what is nowadays Hopei, Shantung, Kiangsu, Chekiang, to Ch'üanchou (Zayton) in Fukien, the most important seaport of Eastern Asia at that period. In 1292 he left China by sea, sailing from Ch'üanchou by way of Indo-China, Java, Ceylon and the west coast of India to Hormuz; and then by land through Persia, Georgia and back by way of the Black Sea and the Mediterranean. In 1295 he found himself once again in his birthplace Venice. Soon afterwards he was taken prisoner in a sea battle between the Venetians and the Genoese and was imprisoned in Genoa. There, in the year 1298 he dictated to the Pisan Rustichello an account of his journey. Rustichello wrote down Marco Polo's words in a mixture of French and Italian. The original is no longer extant, but exists only in a series of later transcriptions and translations which differ from one another. The account bears the title *Description of the World.*

Marco Polo's account is a document of the utmost import-ance. It is one of the most important travel reports that the world has ever known. It revealed to the West a completely new world of which scarcely anything had hitherto been known. Marco Polo saw and described the Mongol Empire, the greatest Empire known to history, at the culmination of its power, and also the Chinese civilisation of the Sung period. In spite of the political weakness of China, its cultural develop-ment at that period was at a very high level. Neither in the West nor in the East was there a country that could be com-pared with the Chinese civilisation at that period for splendour and sophistication.

In the first place, Marco Polo's account contains most important material concerning the Mongol Empire, of which China was of course only a part; and even today it is still a primary historical source. Marco Polo's reliability has been shown by contemporary sources from the Mongol and Chinese side. Amongst other things, Marco Polo described the organ-isation of the state, and the fiscal and monetary system, and the excellent postal and messenger service which extended through-out the whole Empire. But in the course of his journeys he came to know not only North China (Kitai), which had been incorporated into the Mongol Empire since 1234, but also Central and Southern China. He was the first European to describe China from his own observation. Hangchou (Quinsai), the capital of the Southern Sung dynasty conquered by the Mongols in 1279, made a great impression on Marco Polo by its size and magnificence, its elegance and refinement. Two of the longest chapters of his account are devoted to describing it. Here again, the descriptions given in contemporary Chinese sources confirm how accurate and reliable were the observations of Marco Polo; but few of these accounts are as lively and informative as his. It is true that as an official of Khubilai, Marco Polo regarded China predominantly from the Mongol point of view. Thus in the first place he saw the external, material civilisation. He scarcely mentions Chinese intellectual life, religion, philosophy, literature and art. But even without this, the report already contained enough that was completely new to the Europe of his day. Two examples from the description of Hangchou will serve as an example of the precision of Marco Polo's observation:

In other streets are stationed the courtesans, who are in so great number that I dare not say it; and not only near the squares where places are usually assigned to them, but all over the city. And they stay very sumptuously with great perfumes and with many maid-servants, and the houses all decorated. These women are very clever and practised in knowing how to flatter and coax with ready words and suited to each kind of person, so that the foreigners who have once indulged themselves with them stay as it were in an ecstasy, and are so much taken with their sweetness and charms that they can never forget them. And from this it comes to pass that when they return home they say that they have been in Quinsai, that is in the city of Heaven, and never see the hour that they may be able to go back there again. . . .[1]

They have their houses very well built and richly worked, and they take so great delight in ornaments, paintings, and buildings, that the sums they spend on them are a stupendous thing. The native inhabitants of the city of Quinsai are peaceful people through having been so brought up and habituated by their kings, who were of the same nature. They do not handle arms nor keep them at home. Quarrels or any difference are never heard or noticed among them. They do their merchandise

[1] Moule-Pelliot, *Marco Polo, The Description of the World*, 2 Vols. London 1938, I, 328–329.

and arts with great sincerity and truth. They love one another so that a district may be reckoned as one family on account of the friendliness which exists between the men and women by reason of the neighbourhood. So great is the familiarity that it exists between them without any jealousy or suspicion of their women, for whom they have the greatest respect; and one who should dare to speak improper words to any married woman would be thought a great villain. They are equally friendly with the foreigners who come to them for the sake of trade, and gladly receive them at home, saluting them, and give them every help and advice in the business which they do. On the other hand they do not like to see soldiers, nor those of the great Khan's guards, as it seems to them that by reason of them they have been deprived of their natural kings and lords.[1]

Marco Polo met the same fate in his homeland as has befallen many another, both before his time and since, who was the first to discover something new and ahead of his time. No one believed Marco Polo and his accounts of a great and powerful empire in the East with a highly developed civilisation. All this was regarded as fantasy. A few friends advised him to retract his statements. They felt that Marco Polo's descriptions of these marvels were highly entertaining, but that he ought not to put them out as the truth. His story of the ancient and civilised nations of the East and their achievements were irreconcilable with the Christian view of the world at that period, based as it was on dogma. In this view it was inconceivable that there could be another centre of highly developed civilisation outside the Christian world.

Marco Polo's account was soon translated and adapted into other languages. The translators made many arbitrary alterations in the original text, and added a great deal more out of their own imagination. Thus these translations mostly contained collections of fantastic fairy tales suited to the taste of those times. Many of the changes, which amounted to pure fables about journeys which had never been undertaken, gave the most ludicrous and fantastic description of what were supposed to be Chinese customs and usages. Such

[1] Moule-Pelliot I, 330.

fabrications found a wide audience and for the most part were more readily believed than the accurate account given by Marco Polo himself. It was possible to tell the most absurd stories about the wonderland of Cathay, and be believed. Such distorted accounts of foreign nations and their heathen superstitions were popular at that time. They flattered the pride and the cultural self-consciousness of European Christians. Perhaps the roots of the inclination of Europeans to discuss China and everything Chinese with frivolity and sarcastic sniggering, which unfortunately has not yet been completely overcome, may go back to these stories. Marco Polo's discovery perhaps came too soon for Western man. Only a small circle of scholars, first in Italy and then elsewhere, gradually recognised that Marco Polo's account was the truth, and that outside the Christian West there was another vast and highly advanced world. Most people were still far from being able to accept this.

4. THE CHRISTIAN MISSIONS IN MONGOL CHINA

The Mongol emperors were tolerant with regard to religion, though more from indifference than from conviction or magnanimity. Thus within the Mongol Empire, the most various religions had free rein for their activities. Amongst these, Nestorian Christians were of not inconsiderable importance. Nestorian or Chaldaean Christianity had been known in China since the beginning of the 7th century; before the beginning of the Mongol period various nations in Western Mongolia had been Nestorian (e.g. Naiman, Kerait, etc.). Later, people from these nations frequently worked in China as officials. Thus in the Mongol period, Nestorian Christianity was very widespread in China, as is attested by written sources and documents. Through Rubruk and the Polos the news of the religious freedom that obtained in the Mongol Empire, and of the numerous Nestorian Christians, had reached Rome. Consequently, at the end of the 13th century the Pope sent an experienced missionary, the Italian Franciscan Giovanni de

Monte Corvino, into the Mongol Empire. He travelled by sea, by way of India, to the Chinese port of Zayton (Ch'üanchou) and then on to the capital Khanbalik (Peking) where he seems to have had considerable success. A considerable number—more than ten thousand is mentioned—of Tatars were said to have received baptism. With the support of an Italian merchant who was settled in Peking at the time, Monte Corvino was able to obtain a very fine piece of ground for the headquarters of this mission, and to build two churches. Christian communities were founded in Khanbalik, Zayton and at other places. On the basis of the favourable reports he received in 1307 the Pope named Monte Corvino as Archbishop of Khanbalik. At the same time he sent a number of other Franciscans to act as suffragans to Monte Corvino in China. But only three of them ultimately arrived in China, of whom only Andrea de Perugia, the Bishop of Zayton, is known to us.

Unfortunately very little material concerning this early Franciscan mission is still extant. In particular, it is not possible to obtain a picture of missionary practice at that period, nor of the circles from which the members of the Christian communities were drawn. In Europe people liked to imagine that even the Khan himself and his mother had become Christians. The same was later claimed of other Chinese emperors, but it was nothing more than a piece of wishful thinking on the part of the missionaries, which never came to reality. Certainly, the Mongol government does not seem to have hindered the spread of Roman Catholic Christianity in any way; but it seems as though the Nestorians, who were obviously displeased at this competition, sought to create difficulties for the Roman Catholic missionaries and intrigued against them. This is the beginning of the intolerance of different Christian denominations towards one another which was to take on a much more ominous form centuries later. The opposition of the Nestorians, however, seems to have had little success, for the Mongol Khan was generous and impartial towards all religions. Monte Corvino enjoyed great respect in Khanbalik, until he died in 1328 or 1329 at an advanced age. Little is known about his successors, if in fact any such actually took office. The last Franciscan to be sent by the Pope to China was Giovanni de Marignolli, who came to Khanbalik in 1342, but soon returned. For by then, the disturbances which preceded the overthrow of Mongol rule in China had already begun. The Christian communities too did not long survive the end of the Mongol rule. After the foundation of the native Ming Dynasty (1368), which in religious matters was far less tolerant than the Mongols, nothing more is recorded of Christian bodies, neither Roman Catholic nor Nestorian.

The accounts of the Franciscans added much to Europe's knowledge of Eastern Asia as provided by Marco Polo. In particular, the account by the Franciscan friar and traveller Odorico de Pordenone of his journeys, contained interesting accounts of Khanbalik, Zayton, etc., even though they can scarcely be compared with the descriptions of Marco Polo. Odorico, who was active during the third decade of the 14th century in Zayton, came to Khanbalik in 1325, and travelled back to Europe along the land route in 1328.

5. CHINA'S KNOWLEDGE OF EUROPE IN THE MONGOL PERIOD

It is not known whether any Chinese came to Central or Western Europe during the Mongol period. Thus there are no accounts of journeys such as that of Marco Polo. There exist in Chinese only descriptions of journeys in Western Central Asia. It is known, however, that apart from those who have been mentioned, numerous other Europeans spent more or less time in Khanbalik or in other places in China. Thus the Chinese possessed some knowledge of the existence of Europe.

The Mongols were not very interested in intellectual culture, but they were very concerned with material achievements. The powerful Mongol Empire made possible an intensive cultural exchange between China and the Near East to a previously unknown degree. Experts in various fields of natural science and technology travelled between China and the West and exchanged their knowledge and experiences with one another. Thus, during the Mongol period, a valuable stimulus was given in China to astronomy, mathematics, medicine, geography, architecture, the manufacture of fire-arms, etc.

As the result of their extensive conquests in the West, the Mongols had a particular interest in geography. Numerous geographical works on the West were produced. A map of the world drawn by the Chinese Li Tse-min in 1330 surpasses Arabian and European maps of that period. It shows that the Mongols and Chinese of the early 14th century had a far better geographical conception of the world outside China, including the Far West, than Europeans possessed of the central and eastern parts of Asia. Unfortunately the original map of Li Tse-min is no longer extant, but only a Korean copy from the year 1402.[1] The map reaches from Japan to the Azores, and from Africa to Central Russia. It gives about one hundred place names for Europe, including A-lu-mang-ni-a (=Alle-mannia, Allemagne) in the extreme North-West. It gives thirty-five place names in Africa.

[1] The title of the original is *Sheng chiao kuang pei t'u* and of the Korean copy *Hun-i chiang-li li-tai kuo-tu chih t'u*. Cf. Walter Fuchs, *The 'Mongol Atlas' of China*, Peking 1946.

III

The First Direct Contact by Sea between China and Europe

1. The Discovery of China by the Portuguese

In the 15th century, only a few decades before the beginning of the great journeys of discovery by Spanish and Portuguese mariners, the greatest and most far-reaching maritime enterprises of Chinese history took place. Great fleets, consisting of up to sixty-two large ships with over twenty-seven thousand sailors and soldiers, sailed from the Chinese coast through the straits of Malacca, and by way of India, into the Persian Gulf, into the Red Sea, and on to the east coast of Africa. But in 1433 these expeditions came to an end, as suddenly as they had begun thirty years previously. The European seafarers in their turn rounded the Cape of Good Hope in 1497 and pressed on further and further towards the east. In Calicut, on the Indian coast, the Portuguese heard stories of the great fleets which had regularly come there eighty years previously. According to a Portuguese account, these ships were manned by 'white Christians who wore their hair long like the Germans, and had a beard only around their mouths, like the knights and courtiers in Constantinople'. They wore armour, with a helmet and visor, and 'a weapon fastened to a lance'.[1] This description can only refer to the Chinese. For it is not possible that other Europeans could have arrived in such great numbers. Perhaps the Portuguese even met a few descendants of the Chinese of that period.

It was in 1509 that the Portuguese first came to Malacca,

[1] E. Zechlin, 'Die Ankunft der Portugiesen in Indien, China und Japan als Problem der Universalgeschichte', *Historische Zeitschrift* 1938, pp. 491–526, especially pp. 503–516.

whose Sultan at that time still nominally owed tribute to China as a result of the great sea expeditions. The leader of the Portuguese squadron had been given the task by his king of bringing back from Malacca information about the 'Chijns', that is, about the Chinese. At that time Malacca was also much frequented by Chinese merchant ships. This paved the way for the second discovery of China by the West. Of course no one yet knew that this was in fact Marco Polo's Cathay. In 1513—or as other scholars think, in 1514—the first Portuguese, Jorge Alvarez, arrived in China. He landed on the island Ling Ting near T'unmen (the island Tamão, a spit of land near Nant'ou, north-west of what is now Chiulung (Kowloon, opposite Hong Kong) and there he erected a small stone monument with the Portuguese coat-of-arms. This was presumably meant to signify that he was taking possession of the land; in any case that is how the Chinese understood it. Alvarez returned after a short time, and in 1521 set out on a second journey, on which he died soon after his arrival in T'unmen, and was buried beside his monument.

A short time after the first journey of Alvarez in the year 1515, the Portuguese governor of Malacca, Jorge d'Albuquerque, sent Raphael Perestrello 'to discover China'. He travelled on a Chinese ship as far as the Bay of Canton, and reported on his return in the same year 'that the Chinese desired peace and friendship with the Portuguese, and that they were a very good people'.[1]

The first Portuguese expeditions were undertaken by individuals travelling more or less in a private capacity, and not as official representatives of their government. The first truly official Portuguese embassy with several ships of its own, with a letter from the king of Portugal to the 'King of China', and led by Fernão Peres d'Andrade, arrived in the Bay of Canton two years later, in 1517. After some formality and delay they received from the appropriate Chinese officials permission to make their way up river to Canton. Following

[1] Albert Kammerer, *La découverte de la Chine par les Portugais au XVIème siècle et la cartographie des Portulans*, Leiden 1944, p. 14.

their own custom, the Portuguese fired a salute of a few rounds before the city. This was misunderstood by the Chinese. In the first place, they were not acquainted with this custom, and in addition, it was strictly forbidden to carry armaments in the harbour of Canton. This caused considerable agitation amongst the Chinese, and from the beginning the unknown foreigners were met with deep suspicion. Thus began the long series of misunderstandings, mutual mistrust, and contempt, which were to cause so much harm in the future, and which right up to the present time are characteristic of the relations between China and the West.

The impression which this first embassy from a European state made upon the Chinese is reflected in the following description by the Chinese official Ku Ying-hsiang (1483–1565):

In the year Chengte *ting-ch'ou* (1517), when I was secretary of the provincial government in Canton, and was acting as deputy for the commissioner in charge of merchant shipping, there suddenly appeared (one day) two large sea-going ships, which sailed in towards Canton, right up to Huaiyüan-i. They said that they brought tribute from the land Folangchi.[1] The person in charge of their ship was called Chiapitan (Captain). The crew all had prominent noses and deep-set eyes. Their heads were all wrapped round with a white cloth, like the dress of the Mohammedans. I immediately made a report to the Governor General [of the provinces Kuangtung and Kuangsi] Lord Ch'en Hsi-hsüan, with the personal name Chin, who was just staying at Canton. Since these people did not know the rites, I arranged that they should be practised in the ceremonies for three days in Kuanghsiao-szu and then be led to the audience [with the Governor General]. As it is not laid down in the *Collected Statutes of the Ming Empire*, that this land brings tribute, I submitted a complete report on the matter to the throne. When the court had signified its accord, we sent them [to Peking] to the Ministry [of Rites which was responsible for the foreign embassies bringing tribute]. Since at that period the emperor Wu-tsung (Chengte) was on a journey in the south, they remained for a year in the government guest-house for foreign embassies bringing

[1] Folangchi-Faranghi, France. The transmission of this name is not clear. It is implied that the Portuguese themselves first appeared in China under this false name.

tribute (Hui-t'ung kuan). After the present Emperor had ascended
the throne (this was in 1521), on account of their lack of respect
the [Chinese] interpreter was sentenced to death, and these people
returned under escort to Canton. They were deported and sent
away from the country. During their long stay in Canton these
people gladly read Buddhist books.[1]

2. RELATIONS WITH FOREIGN NATIONS IN CHINESE POLITICAL THEORY AND PRACTICE

It is not possible to understand the development of the
relationship between China and the West following the arrival
of the Portuguese in China, with the numerous and complicated
problems involved, without a clear picture of the ideological
and institutional presuppositions about relations with foreigners
which were held by both sides.

According to the cosmic and universalist world view of
classical China, mankind on earth ought to be organised in a
similar way to the ordering of the stars in heaven. Just as in
heaven the Pole Star remained fixed in the centre, and all the
others stars revolved round it, so on earth the central ruler,
the Emperor, ought as the Son of Heaven to be the immovable
pole about which mankind moved. The Emperor stood as a
link between heaven and earth, or between heaven and men.
The dwelling-place of the Emperor, that is, in the narrower
sense, the imperial Residence, and in a wider sense the Middle
Kingdom, *chung-kuo* (the present Chinese name for China), was
the centre of the inhabited world, the source of all culture and
civilisation. Around the Middle Kingdom are grouped the
foreign states, *wai-kuo*. As the distance from the centre
increased, the standard of their culture and civilisation
decreased. The peculiar geographical and ethnic situation of
China made it possible to reconcile this theory, not entirely,
but to a very considerable degree, with reality.

Along all its borders China is surrounded by steppe or
mountains. The pastoral and hunting people who inhabited
these regions were culturally always far inferior to the settled,

[1] Mao Yüan-i, *Wu-pei chih*, 1621/28, ch. 122, 7b–8a.

agricultural Chinese. Thus traditionally China knew no genuine nationalism, but had an outlook which has sometimes been described as 'culturalism'. The Chinese saw their cultural superiority to the barbarians. The Chinese script and literature, Chinese customs and the Chinese way of life, were such unique achievements that all the barbarians who came into contact with them were utterly impressed and sought to acquire something of them. But by adopting the culture and way of life of the Chinese, they became gradually more and more assimilated to them, and finally, abandoning their own original characteristics, became Chinese. In the course of the centuries, the numerous non-Chinese people of the fertile and rich agricultural areas of south and west China became wholly Chinese in this way. At the present day there are only a few remnants of non-Chinese tribes in isolated mountain districts.

In the north it was different. There, the steppe, unsuited to agriculture, soon set bounds to the spread of the Chinese way of life. The highly mobile inhabitants of the steppe, with their cavalry, were often superior to the Chinese in battle. They repeatedly succeeded in overrunning and bringing under their control large parts of north China, and on two occasions the whole of China. But they were never in a position to rule the richly populated arable land by their own resources. For this, they needed the Chinese bureaucracy and its institutions, the detailed organisation of the Chinese system of government. A barbarian could become Chinese Emperor, but only by fitting himself into the Chinese system and largely giving up his own characteristic ways. It is typical of the traditional Confucian state that it could be ruled by foreigners and used by foreigners, but never knew any other state which was on equal terms with itself. There are one or two cases in their history (e.g. Sung and Liao in the 11th century) where it was not possible to avoid the practical recognition of a neighbouring state on equal terms, but a constant and vigorous effort was always made by the Chinese to maintain the theory at least in appearance.

It is true that the Chinese had also come into contact with

the highly developed civilisations of Central Asia and India, as for example through the embassy of Chang Ch'ien in the second century B.C. (see above). Chinese civilisation had also been considerably stimulated and enriched in several vital aspects from India and Central Asia. One has only to think of the introduction of Buddhism from India, with its underlying complex of Indian ideas. But such encounters with other advanced civilisations were never able to alter the Chinese picture of the world in its basic principles, or even to modify it. Thus the pattern of the relationship between the centre, China, and the barbarians living on the periphery took on a definite fixed form. The form in which this relationship was operated was what is called the tribute system, an institution for ordering the intercourse between the Chinese and the barbarians which was recognised by them both. In Chinese thought the tribute system held a similar place to that enjoyed by nationalism and international law in Western thought during the 19th century.

According to the Chinese conception, the Chinese Emperor ruled in virtue of his superior human qualities and his all-embracing favour, which was equally to be enjoyed by all men, both Chinese and barbarian. In order to receive this imperial favour and to succeed in enjoying the blessings of Chinese civilisation, it was supposed that the most distant and uncivilised barbarians would come to the Chinese imperial court 'to be transformed' (lai-hua). And in fact they did come. They sent embassies with gifts, that is, embassies to pay tribute. The embassies were received as guests in the Chinese capital and received gifts in return, which were worth at least the same amount, and often more, than what the foreigners had brought. This generosity was usually an expression of magnanimous condescension, but was sometimes an agreed payment by China to appease a militarily powerful neighbour. The visit of an embassy took place according to a detailed and subtly elaborated ceremonial culminating in a solemn reception by the Emperor. What is called the kotow, the three-fold genuflection with the touching of the ground nine times with the foreheads, played an important part in this. The question of the kotow later gave rise to considerable conflicts when ambassadors arrived from the West. In the patriarchal and hierarchical Chinese ordering of society, it was a natural expression of reverence towards older persons and those of higher social rank. Even the Chinese Emperor carried out the kotow before his symbolic ancestors Heaven and Earth, and also before the memorial tablets of his earthly forefathers. The bringing of tribute and the ceremonial related to it signified for the Chinese that the barbarians recognised the superiority of China and the suzerainty of the Chinese Emperor. At the same time, China only attempted to make this suzerainty felt in practice with the nations who were her immediate neighbours, and even this was done to varying degrees. Thus for example, from the beginning of the eighteenth century Mongolia and Tibet were annexed to China in a much more real sense than countries such as Korea, Annam or Laos. In the case of distant countries such as Nepal or Malacca Chinese suzerainty remained for the most part purely theoretical. As a rule, the Chinese made no attempt to become involved in the internal affairs of a foreign nation or country. There were other countries, such as Japan, which were regarded as tribute states by the Chinese; Japan even had embassies with tribute at certain times, but otherwise decisively rejected the claim to suzerainty of the Chinese Emperor. Often the embassies bringing tribute were accompanied by merchants, who were permitted, within a strictly defined area and under fixed conditions, to trade in China with the goods they had brought with them and to exchange them for Chinese goods. The frequency of the embassies from each individual country, and the number of ambassadors, of persons accompanying them, and of merchants, was laid down exactly.

This tribute system had been developed by the Chinese in the course of the centuries principally in their relationship with the peoples of the Central Asian steppe. With them, as also with China's neighbours to the south and south-west, it had been carefully kept in force. For the Chinese, this system

C

was quite simply the only imaginable way of conducting relations with foreign nations. But it was completely unfitted for use in their dealings with the nationalistic and industrialised countries of the West. In spite of this, up to the end of the 19th century, the Chinese attempted by every possible means to fit their relationships with European countries into the categories of the tribute system. For the Chinese, trade formed part of the tribute system. According to the Chinese point of view it had no independent significance in itself, and was only a phenomenon which accompanied a political act. A limited trade could be graciously permitted to the barbarians as a means whereby they could share in the riches and the achievements of China. Over and above the activities of the embassies that brought tribute, trade could sometimes be permitted at certain borderposts or ocean ports. But permission to trade was always a gracious concession on the part of the Chinese, and for the foreigners to claim the right to trade was unthinkable according to Chinese ideas. For the Chinese, the essential thing was the political and ideal significance of tribute; for the Europeans what mattered was the material value of the trade. An attitude to trade similar to that which at present obtains in China has a very ancient tradition behind it. A further result of this view of trade was that apart from the maritime expeditions at the beginning of the 15th century (cf. Ch. III, §1 above), which were altogether unique, the Chinese government was always opposed to overseas enterprises by Chinese merchants, and sometimes actually tried to prevent them by force. Foreigners could come to China to bring tribute; but it was not the wish of the government that Chinese should go out to the barbarians. Thus apart from the extraordinarily significant colonisation of districts bordering directly on China and of foreign enclaves (see above), the Chinese—at least after the 8th century A.D.—never showed any interest in carrying the Chinese way of life into foreign countries and propagating it there, as did the Islamic nations, or later, the nations of the West.

It is not necessary to go into detail concerning the fundamental attitude of the Europeans of the 16th century, which is already well known. The Portuguese set out in the spirit of Crusaders to fight against their immediate enemies, the Moslems, and to convert the heathen. Alongside this, trade and the related expectation of profit played an ever more important part. From the very beginning, the Portuguese held the view later shared by all Europeans, that only Europeans had the right to sail the seas and control them. The definite legal norms which were developed were only for use amongst Europeans, and had no validity for Asian and African nations. This view could not fail to come into conflict with that of the Chinese. The report of Ku Ying-hsiang quoted above (Ch. III, §1) suggests this. Even more serious disputes were to follow.

3. The Expulsion of the Portuguese and the Prohibition of Trade

The description quoted above (Ch. III, §1) of the arrival of the Portuguese embassy of 1517 also included the events of the following years. Apart from the inappropriate salute fired in Canton, the first Portuguese behaved in a relatively restrained way and took care to provoke no clash with the Chinese. A change took place, however, in the summer of 1519, when Simão d'Andrade, probably a brother or cousin of Fernão Peres d'Andrade, landed with a few ships at T'unmen. Simão d'Andrade and his followers behaved in an arrogant and brutal way like conquerors, refused to follow the 'orders given' by the Chinese authorities, and harassed the local population. Following the custom which had proved profitable in Africa, they went so far as to take captives in order to carry them away as slaves. They seemed to have concentrated on adolescent youths and girls, some of whom they captured, and others of whom they bought. As a result the story spread amongst the Chinese, who were always ready to recount horrific tales about uncivilised barbarians, that the Portuguese took or bought children in order to toast and eat them. This cannibalism was portrayed in great detail. In later times, Europeans were repeatedly represented by the Chinese as cannibals. In consequence of the behaviour of the Europeans, which was frequently brutal, and was always felt by the Chinese to be uncivilised and savage, such stories were widely believed.

As has been said, the embassy of 1517 brought with it to Canton a letter from the King of Portugal to the Chinese Emperor. Not until three years later, in 1520, after the fleet under Fernão Peres d'Andrade had long since sailed away, did Thomé Pires, who had been selected to deliver the letter to the Chinese emperor, receive permission to travel to Nanking and then to Peking. There it was established that the information previously received from Canton was false, and that the letter of the King of Portugal was arrogant and unseemly. In the meantime the news of the behaviour of Simão d'Andrade and his followers had reached Peking. The result was that Pires was not received by the Emperor, the acceptance of the gift was refused, and the letter of the King of Portugal was burnt. The Chinese interpreter was executed and the members of the embassy were sent back to Canton as prisoners. In the autumn of 1521 they arrived there, but remained in custody. In 1524 Pires died in prison. In the meantime further disagreements with the Portuguese had taken place, the final result of which was that from 1522 the Portuguese were forbidden to return to China. Trade with them was prohibited, and appropriate military precautions were taken to ensure that these measures were carried out if the Portuguese should resist. Thus the direct link between China and the West was temporarily brought to an end.

As a further illustration, here is a second Chinese description of this first encounter between the Portuguese and the Chinese, so symptomatic of the further development of relations between China and the West:

The Portuguese [here: Folangchi] had not previously had any dealings with China. In the year Chengte 12 [1517] they suddenly arrived in great ships in the anchorage of Canton. The noise of their cannons was like thunder. They declared that they were bringing tribute, and wished to ask for the granting of a feudal title. The administration commissioner of the right and surveillance vice-commissioner, Wu T'ing-chü, gave them permission to bring tribute. The censorial inspectors established that in the *Collected Statutes* there was no precedent [for a tribute-embassy from the Portuguese] and did not permit them to go [to the capital]. So they returned and anchored at Nant'ou near Tungkuan. They at once built houses [there], put up palisades and relied on their fire arms to secure their [position]. When some of them came to the Ministry [of Rites] they did not carry out the kneeling ceremony, and for the audience at the imperial court they claimed precedence before all other barbarians.

The censors Ch'iu Tao-lung and Ho Ao in turn prepared detailed memoranda. [In them] they said that [the Portuguese] regarded violence and insurrection as courage, that they had driven out the princes of their own country, and that they had sent in advance Ḥōja Asan (Huo-che Ya-san) who had falsely described himself as an ambassador sent from Malacca. Overtaken by a storm [the Portuguese] had arrived at the Anchorage [of Canton]; they went about reconnoitring, and made themselves familiar with our roads and streets; they stole or bought little children in order to cook and eat them. Recently the king of Malacca reported in a memorandum that they had taken his land away from him and killed [many men] in enmity. The harm they caused by their killing and plundering was without parallel. It consequently seemed proper to send [the Portuguese] away at once, strictly to forbid private trade with them, and to destroy without trace the houses and fortifications they had built; the prosecution and punishment of merchants and craftsmen who were carrying on private trade with the barbarians was to be intensified. An imperial edict approved these suggestions. . .[1]

The essential point is not whether all the allegations in this report are in fact true—in part they are not—nor is it necessary to go into them in detail. What is of decisive importance is the view taken by the Chinese of that period of the Europeans, as it is expressed in this account. And it must not be supposed that the facts are consciously being distorted here; rather, the

[1] Ku Yen-wu, *T'ien-hsia chün-kuo li-ping shu*, 1662, ch. 119, 53a–b; Shorter version in Chang Hsieh, *Tung hsi-yang k'ao*, 1618, ch. 5, 7a. Translated by P. Pelliott in *T'oung Pao*, 38, 1948, p. 127–128.

description given is simply what the author was convinced was the case.

4. FURTHER DEVELOPMENTS UP TO THE END OF THE MING DYNASTY (1644)

Trade brought profit equally to the Portuguese and to Chinese merchants and officials—through bribery and other illegal revenue—and it could not be permanently suppressed. When Canton was closed, it first shifted northward to the ports of Ch'üanchou and Changchou in Fukien and Ningpo in Chekiang. There the control was less strict. Of course the Portuguese carefully avoided drawing attention to themselves by appearing in great numbers in the ports, in order not to damage the facilities for trade in these places as well. Gradually, however, the circumstances grew more favourable for a resumption of trade even in Canton. As early as 1530 Canton was formally reopened to foreign trade; but the Portuguese were still expressly excluded from the port because of their previous bad behaviour. They themselves did not attempt to return to Canton, but remained content with the temporary foothold obtained during the fifth decade of the century in less populous places or on islands at the entrance to the Bay of Canton. They finally succeeded in 1557 in founding a fixed depot on a small unhabited peninsula at the entrance to the Bay of Canton called Macao, in Chinese Aomen or Haoching, and this developed rapidly in the years that followed. As a result of their previous unfortunate experiences, the Portuguese restrained themselves and tried to remain on good terms with the Chinese authorities, who as a result let the Portuguese do as they wished. The Chinese were happy not to have the troublesome foreigners in Canton itself, but at the same time to profit both officially and privately from the rich customs revenues of the Portuguese trade in Macao. The moderate approach of the Portuguese to the Chinese officials, as well as presents made at appropriate moments, had the required effect. There is no evidence for the suggestion later put forward by the

Portuguese, that they had received Macao as a thank-offering for their help in destroying pirates. Nevertheless, it is possible that the Portuguese took part in battles against the very numerous pirates, even though it is hardly likely that the Chinese would have permitted them their depot in Macao for this reason alone. It may have been easier for the Chinese authorities to tolerate the presence of the Portuguese in Macao in view of the fact that as long as they were there they were very much in the hands of the Chinese. Macao is joined to the mainland by a very narrow isthmus, and food supplies can be cut off at once by closing it.

In accordance with Chinese tradition, the barbarians were permitted, within their depot or the area inhabited by them, to live according to their own customs and their own law. The Chinese authorities maintained formal relations with the head of the barbarians, called in Macao and also elsewhere *I-mu*, literally "the barbarians" eye'. This leader was given a nominal Chinese official rank, and was responsible to the Chinese authorities for the maintenance of order in the depot, and for the good behaviour of its inhabitants outside the depot— where they were permitted to leave it at all. This institution for the government of foreign elements in the population which had not adopted Chinese ways, through their own tribal chieftains and in accordance with their own laws and customs, had long been used by the Chinese with success in dealing with the numerous non-Chinese aboriginal people within China. The trading depots of the Arabs and Persians, which existed from the 8th to the 12th century in a number of coastal towns in Southern China, had also possessed their own administration in the same way. In Chinese eyes this was not a special privilege granted to the foreigners, or to which they had a legitimate claim. It rather implies a certain contempt for them: the barbarians were regarded as unable to understand the civilised customs and sophisticated way of life of the Chinese; thus they were obliged to live in their own primitive and barbarian way! But it was naturally expected that in general they would take their place within the Chinese system. The Chinese also always regarded the territory of a foreign depot as a part of China, in which the foreigners had simply been permitted to live for a while. In the case of the toleration of the Portuguese depot in Macao there can be no doubt that the Chinese authorities regarded Macao as still part of Chinese territory, remaining under their authority. The Portuguese in their turn were glad to be able to live according to their own laws and customs, and carefully refrained from contradicting the Chinese view. It is important in this matter to appreciate the original Chinese conception, in order to understand the conflicts which arose later, in the 19th century, concerning foreign depots and extra-territorial jurisdiction between China and the Western powers.

The first great period of prosperity in Macao, during which the Portuguese possessed a virtual monopoly in maritime trade with China, did not last beyond the end of the 16th century. Even before the turn of the century, the Spaniards came from Manila, and in 1601 the Dutch reached China. They came into immediate conflict with the Portuguese, who saw their monopoly threatened by the newcomers. The Portuguese seized the vessels of their unwelcome competitors, and in some cases cruelly murdered their crews. Those who suffered these attacks plotted vengeance, and returned violence for violence. This behaviour only strengthened the Chinese in their contempt for the brutal and uncivilised barbarians, particularly as the Portuguese even tried to intrigue with the Chinese authorities against their competitors. The Chinese, of course, quickly realised the intention of the Portuguese and took little notice of it. It had always been Chinese policy to treat all barbarians equally and to permit them all to enjoy the blessings of Chinese civilisation—in this case by permitting them to trade—to the same extent. This of course did not prevent them from playing off one barbarian nation against another, or even, in case of necessity, from letting them destroy each other. Thus here again, the attitude of the Chinese may well have encouraged rather than prevented the battles between the competitors. Chinese distrust of the Portuguese grew; and

Macao and its Portuguese trade experienced greater and greater difficulties. In addition to the Dutch and Spaniards, the year 1625 brought the British to compete with the Portuguese for trade. The disturbances during the last two decades before the fall of the Ming Dynasty likewise caused the decline of trade. And the growing ascendency of the British and Dutch over the Portuguese and Spaniards also brought an end to the Portuguese predominance in the trade with China. Thus Macao gradually declined into insignificance.

To sum up, it can be said of this period in the relationship between China and the West, that the general attitude of European mariners and merchants, as well as the conflicts, jealousies and intrigues which they conducted towards one another, brought down on them from the very beginning the contempt, aversion and hostility of the Chinese. Furthermore, as a result of the thoroughgoing dogmatising of Confucian teaching and the greater isolation of China from the outside world, Chinese official and literary circles at that time were very much more exclusive and narrow-minded than had been the case at the time of the Arab and Persian trading depots from the 8th to the 12th century. Thus the relationship between China and the West was ill-fated from the beginning.

IV

The First Intellectual Contact between
China and the West

1. THE BEGINNING OF THE JESUIT MISSION: MATTEO RICCI

As has already been said (see Ch. II, §2 above) the conversion
of the heathen to Christianity was *one* of the main impulses for
the great voyages of discovery carried out by the Portuguese,
and for their founding of colonies. Thus it was obvious that
merchants would also be followed by missionaries in China.
The first attempt of Catholic missionaries to gain admission
into China, however, was in vain. In 1552 the 'Apostle of
Japan' the Spaniard Francis Xavier, landed on a small island in
the Bay of Canton. But he died there in the same year, without
being able to fulfil his most ardent desire, to set foot on China
proper. Three years later, in 1555, the Portuguese priest
Melchoir Nunez Barreto, also a Jesuit, became the first missionary to reach Canton, and remained there for two months. His
primary concern was the pastoral care of the Portuguese who
were held prisoner by the Chinese in Canton, and he tried—
although without success—to obtain their release. Barreto did
not understand Chinese, and was consequently unable to work
amongst the Chinese. He was followed by other Jesuits, and
also by Dominicans, Augustinians and Franciscans. On the
whole they were obliged to limit their activity to Macao. In
spite of repeated attempts, none of them was able to obtain a
firm foothold in China beyond the length of a short visit, or to
begin missionary work amongst the Chinese.

The true founder of the Chinese mission, and also the most
important figure in its whole history, was Matteo Ricci (1552–
1610), an Italian Jesuit who was called in Chinese Li Ma-tou,
with the courtesy name Hsi-t'ai. In 1582 he arrived in Macao

and in the following year obtained permission from the Governor-General of Kuangtung and Kuangsi, to settle with his compatriot and fellow Jesuit Michele Ruggieri in Chaoch'ing (Kaoyao), at that time the seat of the Governor-General on the Western River (Sikiang) a little way above Canton. In 1585 they were both obliged to move to Chaochou in the north of the province Kuangtung. In 1595 Ricci arrived for the first time in the southern capital Nanking, but was not able to remain there, and returned to Nanch'ang, the capital of the Kiangsi Province, on the Yangtse. In 1598 he paid his first short visit to Peking. In the following year he succeeded in settling permanently in Nanking, and finally, in 1601, he was able to move to the actual capital Peking, and to remain there until his death in 1610. Other Jesuits were able to follow him to the different mission stations while he was still alive. The first solemn baptism of a Chinese took place in 1584 in Chaoch'ing. From then on, the number of Chinese Christians grew slowly at first, but constantly, to twenty in the year 1585, forty in the years immediately following, and over a hundred ten years later, in 1596. A decade later, in 1605, there were more than one thousand, in 1615 there were five thousand, and in 1617 there were already about thirteen thousand. In 1636, out of a population of about 150 million there were reckoned to be 38,200 Christians in China. In order to understand properly what these dates signify, it is necessary to realise the enormous difficulties which faced the missionaries in their work, and how Ricci and the Jesuits gradually managed to overcome them.

Ricci recognised very quickly that the essential at first was not to obtain the greatest possible number of conversions and baptisms, but to begin by obtaining for the missionaries a firm and respected position in the social structure of China. A condition of this was a profound study of Chinese customs, language and civilisation, a thorough knowledge of which was in Ricci's view essential if there was to be any hope of successful missionary work. It was infinitely more difficult to obtain such knowledge than at the present day, for no one at that time had the remotest idea of the nature of Chinese civilisation, there were no text-books or other aids to the study of the Chinese language and writings, and one had to rely exclusively on the help of native informants, who at first probably did not even belong to the educated class. For what man of rank and education would have anything to do with the universally despised, uneducated and rootless foreigners! Ricci's unusual talent, his unique insight into people's nature, and particular adaptability, however, made it possible for him to achieve his aim, where almost anyone else would have failed. He succeeded not only in learning the colloquial language very quickly, but also in obtaining an increasing knowledge of the literary language and therefore of the Confucian Canonic Writings, essential to the understanding of Chinese society and its culture.

In their ignorance of the structure of Chinese society Ricci and the Jesuits first of all adopted the dress of the Buddhist priests—this seemed to them to be the most obvious choice. But as his insight into Chinese life increased, Ricci soon noticed that the social standing of Buddhist priests at that time was comparatively inferior. From his knowledge of the bureaucratic structure of Chinese society, Ricci drew the necessary consequence that only a close link with the ruling literary and official class of the *Shen-shih*—and if possible with its upper and highest grades—could provide the missionaries with a relatively respected and assured status in China. Thus Ricci and the Jesuits made the change from the external clothing of Buddhist priests to that of the *Shen-shih*, and they also assimilated their behaviour and deportment to a large extent to that of the *Shen-shih*. Besides this, Ricci sought to penetrate more and more deeply into Confucian teaching. Thus he was able not only to discuss with highly educated scholar-officials all the problems which preoccupied them, but was also able to expound the philosophical and scientific knowledge he had obtained in Europe in a form acceptable to an educated Chinese, and so act as a stimulus. Thus he won the respect and admiration of the leading intellectual circles and was able to make a number of friends amongst their ranks, and later, in many cases, even to win them for Christian baptism. The adoption of Chinese culture was the only way to change the traditional attitude of contempt which the Chinese *Shen-shih* was accustomed to adopt in dealing with barbarians, into recognition and respect. Ricci's gentle and kindly nature, moreover, played its part in winning the affection of many important Chinese personalities. One of his fellow Jesuits later characterised him in the following words:

> Mattheo Riccio, an Italian, so like the Chinese in everything that he seemed to be one of them in the beauty of his countenance, and in the tenderness, gentleness and meekness which they esteem so highly.[1]

While Ricci for his part strove to achieve a very thorough assimilation to Chinese ways, it can also safely be assumed that the extraordinary power of assimilation displayed by Chinese civilisation was not without its effect upon Ricci.

Thus by building up his contact with the highest officials, Ricci was able, in spite of much hostility and resistance, and after careful preparation, to obtain a firm foothold first in Nanking and ultimately in Peking. He was actually invited to an audience with the Emperor, who displayed great interest in the presents Ricci brought with him—especially the clocks with a striking mechanism, and images of the Virgin Mary. The Emperor granted him a pension and permitted him to live permanently in Peking. After his death he was buried near the gate of the city. Since he had gained the favour of the Emperor and the highest officials, the whole bureaucracy which was dependent on them treated him with respect and civility. All this was something quite out of the ordinary for a foreigner, and was previously virtually unknown. It is true that during the Mongol period numerous foreigners worked in China in the service of the Mongol Khan—for example, Marco Polo. But from the beginning of the Ming period the cosmopolitan spirit of the Mongol period had in many respects to

---

[1] P. Sanchez, in Johannes Bettray, *Die Akkomodationsmethode des Paters Matteo Ricci*, Rome 1956, p. XXX.

give way to a reaction which was hostile to foreigners, and to a spirit of narrow orthodoxy. China had isolated herself more and more from the outside world, and every foreigner at once invited suspicion and mistrust. The achievement of Ricci is all the greater, in that without the support of any political power, and without being an accredited ambassador bringing tribute, but entirely on the basis of his cultured and compelling personality, and his infinite patience and adaptability, he obtained access to the highest officials and to the imperial court.

As a scholar and personality, Ricci left behind him a powerful impression on all educated Chinese with whom he came into contact. This is confirmed by numerous surviving accounts by Chinese scholars. As an example, we give a description of Ricci by Li Chih, better known as Li Cho-wu (1527–1602). Li Chih was a very well-known and independent-minded scholar of the period. He had met Ricci in Nanking and in a letter to a friend wrote concerning him as follows:

You have asked me about Li Hsi-t'ai (Ricci's Chinese name). Hsi-t'ai is a man from the Far West. [From there] to China the distance is more than a hundred thousand *li*. He first sailed across the sea to India, and had already travelled more than forty thousand *li* when he first learnt of the existence of the Buddha. It was not until he had reached Canton in the region of the lower course of the Western River, that he learnt that in the country of our great Ming Dynasty there once lived [the legendary rulers of the earliest days] Yao and Shun, and after them the Duke of Chou and Confucius. He lived for almost twenty years at Chaoch'ing in the region of the lower course of the Western River, and read the entire literature of our country. He addressed himself to scholars, so that they could explain to him the pronunciation and meaning of the texts; he went to such as were acquainted with the teachings concerning human nature and reason in the Four Classical Books, so that they could explain the great principles contained therein. Again, he went to those who knew the interpretation of the Six Canonical Writings, so that they could convey their expositions of them to him. Now he has perfectly mastered the art of speaking in our language, and of writing with our script, comporting himself according to our rules of behaviour. He is an extraordinarily impressive person. His mind is lucid and his appearance is simple. When a company of ten or a dozen people are involved in an argument, and each is defending his own view against the other, he stands at one side and does not allow himself to be provoked into intervening, and to become confused. Amongst all the men I have seen, none can compare to him. All who are either too arrogant or too anxious to please, who either display their own cleverness or are too ignorant and dull, are inferior to him. But I do not know how it is that he came here. I have already been with him three times, and still do not know why he has come here. It would be more than foolish if it were perhaps his wish to alter our docrine of the Duke of Chou and of Confucius on the basis of his doctrine. I believe that this is not [the reason why he is here].[1]

The words with which Li Chih concludes his description raise the question of how Ricci tried to put forward Christian doctrine. He did not describe himself in a self-conscious way as a missionary, but constantly emphasised that in the first place he had come to China in order to study the teachings of the wise men of China, and to share in the blessings of Chinese civilisation. He wanted to become Chinese. In this, he was able to approach very closely to the Chinese outlook, and was able to share the same starting point with his partner in a dialogue. It was only then that he revealed his intention of proclaiming the word of God—not so much in opposition to the Confucian tradition but as far as possible in harmony with it. Thus he laid stress on all the ideas in the Canonical Writings which could be brought into accord with Christianity—and these are not a few. He decisively opposed only Buddhism and Taoism. In this, he was able to appeal for support to a number of Confucian thinkers of the past. He cast his arguments in the terminology and form of the Canonical Writings, even though he sometimes departed from the interpretation of later orthodox commentaries. For example, the concepts he used to signify the Christian God, 'Lord of heaven' (*t'ien-chu*) and 'highest ruler' (*shang-ti*) are drawn from the Canonical Writings. But Ricci sought to spread Christian teaching in China not as

---

[1] Jung Chao-tsu, *Li Cho-wu p'ing chuan*, Shanghai 1937, p. 40.

something new and alien, but as something largely in accord with the fundamental principles of Confucian teaching. He sought to adapt Catholicism to the Chinese mentality. He also considered that the Confucian veneration of ancestors and the cult of Confucius, as well as many other Chinese rites, could be reconciled with Christianity—in complete contrast to the nineteenth century missionaries.

Ricci sought to carry out his task not only through the spoken word, but also by his writings. It was very easy to spread the printed word in China. His writings on philosophical and religious subjects, as also on scientific matters, found a wide circulation. Furthermore, many came to visit him, for discussion with him. Thus it came about that the details of his life have been handed down in numerous Chinese historical works. And up to the beginning of the present century Ricci was far better known amongst educated circles in China than in Europe. Only during the last forty years has the West once again remembered this most important mediator between China and the West.

The significance of Ricci, however, does not lie only in the fact that he brought Western ideas to China. It is he who at the same time revealed the intellectual world of China to Europe. Marco Polo was the first to tell Europe of the political organisation and of the material civilisation of the great empire of Eastern Asia. Then the two Portuguese, Galeote Pereira and Gaspar da Cruz—the latter a Dominican friar—and the Spanish Augustinian Martin de Rada published between 1560 and 1580 the first accounts devoted solely to China, on the basis of a short stay in that country. They supplemented the knowledge of China in Europe in particular by observations concerning the daily life and the customs and usages of the Chinese, which are not to be found in Marco Polo. They were also able to give some account of Chinese writings and Chinese literature. De Rada even obtained a number of Chinese books. Marco Polo had hardly been able to relate anything about Chinese intellectual life; and even in the two Portuguese writers, and in de Rada, there is comparatively little on the subject. Their stay in the country was too short for this, and they lacked the necessary contacts with educated Chinese. Thus the discovery of the intellectual civilisation of China was left to Matteo Ricci. We shall have more to say about this later (cf. §5 below); but there is one point that should be mentioned here.

We have already noted that Rubruk rightly identified Kitai and Seres (Ch. II, §2 above). In 1575 or 1576 Martin de Rada wrote that China must be identical with Marco Polo's Cathay. Yet even at the beginning of the seventeenth century, it was supposed in the West that Kitai and Sina or China were two different countries, and it was considered, in fact, that Kitai lay north of China, somewhere in the region of Mongolia. All China was equated with Marco Polo's Manzi. Ricci— presumably without any knowledge of de Rada's comment— correctly presumed that in reality Kitai was identical with Sina or China, and Khanbalik with Peking, but was not able to demonstrate this. The question interested other members of the Order for reasons both of intellectual curiosity and practical use. So the Portuguese lay-brother, Benedict de Goëz, was sent from India to Kitai along the land route described by Marco Polo and the Mohammedans. He was intended to confirm whether or not this route led to China, as it had been made known by Ricci and the other Jesuits with its capital at Peking. In October 1602 de Goëz left Agra in northern India with a caravan, travelled by way of Lahore, Kabul and Samarkand, and crossed the Pamir to Yarkand in East Turkestan and travelled on from there through Turfan and Hami to the Chinese border pass of Chiayükuan. At the end of 1605 he finally arrived in Suchou (in Kansu Province in North-West China), from where, however, he was not permitted to continue his journey to Peking. After a great deal of trouble he finally succeeded in getting a letter to Ricci in Peking. On receiving this, Ricci immediately sent a Chinese lay-brother to Suchou, to make it possible for Goëz to continue his journey to Peking. But Goëz succumbed in Suchou to the enormous hardships of the journey, and in 1607 the Chinese brother was only able to bring a final comfort to the dying man. Only fragments

D

remain of Goëz's account of his journey. Most of it can only
have been transmitted orally to Ricci in Peking by the Armen-
ian who accompanied and survived him. But Goëz's sacrifice
was not in vain. By his daring journey he had shown the
identity of Kitai and Sina or China, and stands as a result in the
foremost rank of the great Portuguese discoverers.

2. RICCI'S SUCCESSORS UP TO THE END OF THE MING
DYNASTY (1644)

The Jesuit mission was able to go on developing and
spreading on the foundations laid by Ricci. It is true that there
were sometimes setbacks, for which the missionaries were not
always without blame. Not all the Jesuit fathers were so
adaptable, tactful and patient as Ricci. But every departure
from the reticent approach so emphatically recommended by
Ricci was paid for sooner or later. Time and again Jesuits
were imprisoned or sent out of the country, and they even had
to abandon their headquarters in Peking for a number of
years. But thanks to the help and intervention on their behalf
of several very influential leading officials, who had become
Christians, all the difficulties were finally overcome. The
private estates of their powerful friends near Shanghai, in
Chekiang and Kiangsi in many cases provided a refuge for the
Jesuit Fathers, when they were banished from other places as
a result of persecution. Perhaps the most important of these
friends was Hsü Kuang-ch'i (Dr. Paul Hsü, 1562–1633), a
scholar who produced many works and was one of the most
influential politicians of that period. His rise to political
power from the middle of the second decade of the 17th
century on, led him in 1632 as far as the highest office, that of
Grand Secretary. He and the group of Christian officials
associated with him definitively assured the status of the Jesuits
during the last two decades of the Ming Dynasty. By their
knowledge of mathematics and astronomy—it was at this time
that European natural science was beginning to overtake that
of China in many fields—as well as by numerous other abilities,

as for example the manufacture of cannon, which were so urgently needed in the struggle of the Dynasty against enemies within and outside the Empire, soon made the learned and dynamic Jesuit Fathers indispensable at the imperial court. In the reign of the last Ming Emperor in particular, the missionaries succeeded in bringing to the Christian faith several of the palace eunuchs, and gradually, with their help, no less than fifty of the ladies of the Inner Palace. It is true that the missionaries did not avoid making enemies. But they shared this fate with all Chinese officials who enjoyed the favour of the Emperor and were consequently exposed to the envy and the jealousy of the others.

A very skilful reaction to the political situation, which no doubt was the correct one from their point of view, made it possible for the Jesuits to survive the confusion in the years that followed, with the fall of the Ming Dynasty and the rise to power of the Manchus, without any great setbacks for the mission. The Order did not throw in its lot on principle with one side or the other, but left it to individual Fathers to adhere to one side or other according to their particular local circumstances at any given time. Thus after the fall of Peking some of them still remained with those who were left of the Ming rulers, who sought, albeit in vain, to restore the Ming Dynasty from Southern China. There were particularly close connections with Christianity amongst the supporters of the Prince of Kuei (Kuei wang), who for a time in the fifth decade of the 17th century, ruled large parts of Southern China; the title of his reign was Yungli. Amongst others at the court of this prince, the leading minister Ch'ü Shih-szu (cf. below) and one of the chief eunuchs, Achilles P'ang (P'ang T'ien-shou), were Christians. On the basis of this association the German Jesuit Father Andreas Wolfgang (or Xavier) Koffler succeeded in baptising a considerable number of the members of the Prince's family including his mother, if not the Prince himself. His mother and the eunuch Achilles P'ang wanted to establish a direct link with the Pope and the Superior-General of the Jesuits, in order to ask for their help against the Manchus.

They sent the Polish Father Michael Boym to Rome as their ambassador, with a letter to this effect. The letter took a long time to answer, and in the meantime the position of the adherents to the Ming Dynasty became completely hopeless, a fact that had also become known in Rome. It was not for another three years, in 1655, that Boym was sent back. The prince of Kuei had had to withdraw to Yünnan in the extreme South-West. Father Boym did return to China, but died before he could reach the Ming Prince and hand over to him the non-committal answer from Rome. This is not historically a very important episode; but it is particularly interesting in that most of the relevant documents are still extant. We shall have to return to it later in another context.

3. THE HEYDAY OF THE MISSION AT THE BEGINNING OF THE MANCHU DYNASTY

The Catholic mission experienced its greatest success under the two first Emperors of the Manchu Ch'ing dynasty, Shun-chih (1644–1661) and K'anghsi (1662–1722). To an even greater extent than at the time of Matteo Ricci, the respect and standing which a few dominant personalities amongst the missionaries possessed at the imperial court, made missionary work possible in Peking and in the provinces. What Ricci had striven for, but had not succeeded in obtaining, a direct personal link with the Emperor, was achieved a few decades later by his successors. The first to obtain this success was the Jesuit Johann Adam Schall von Bell, known in Chinese as T'ang Jo-wang. Under the last Ming Emperor, Adam Schall had already won the favour of the court by his knowledge of astronomy, and through the manufacture of cannon.

According to the Chinese view, what took place in the world was of cosmic significance, and consequently the observation of the stars of heaven and the interpretation of their movements was of the greatest importance. Their purpose was to ensure the harmony of what took place on earth with events in the cosmos, and if need be to prescribe action by the government to avoid irregularities in heaven as a result of abuses on earth. Thus from the earliest times, great importance was accorded in China to the calendar and to the knowledge of astronomy on which it was based. Astronomy and the calculation of the calendar had reached a very high state of development in China at a very early period and were brought to their highest points in the 12th and 13th centuries. After the 14th century, however, no more progress was made, and in fact there was a decline. Consequently, the Jesuits, who were well acquainted with the most recent European studies in this field, showed themselves superior to the Chinese. By predicting eclipses of the sun more accurately than the official Chinese astronomers, the Jesuits were repeatedly able to give a clear demonstration of the greater accuracy and effectiveness of their methods, and thereby to win the respect of every unprejudiced person at the court. In spite of this, as Dr. Joseph Needham has recently established, the effect of the Jesuits on the development of science in China was not entirely advantageous, but in some respects held it back. Sometimes they opposed with false hypotheses Chinese views which were closer to the scientific truth than those of the Jesuits. Thus, for example, the Jesuits emphatically supported the geocentric Ptolemaic and Aristotelian theory, and opposed the heliocentric doctrine of Copernicus, which was closer to the Chinese teaching of the movement of the heavenly bodies in infinite space.

For the reasons given, the exact fixing of the calendar was of decisive importance for a new Dynasty. Irregularities and inaccuracies in the calendar were bound to be regarded as a bad omen for the new government. Besides, as they were foreigners themselves, the Manchus regarded the alien Europeans with less reserve than the Chinese. Thus in the year in which they came to power (1645) the new Manchu government decided to appoint Adam Schall to be in charge of the Department of Astronomy (*Ch'in t'ien chien*). His original refusal was ignored, so that he finally found himself obliged either to risk the whole position of the mission or to accept.

He decided to accept, with the approval of the superiors. Thus he became a state official and a member of the ruling bureaucratic class, with all the associated rights and duties. Although Schall could not compare with Ricci in his Chinese literary education, nevertheless he mastered the language and to a considerable extent the script. Apart from this, he had to make himself fully acquainted with every detail of the complicated official and courtly ceremonial, and adapt himself to the customs of Chinese officialdom.

His new official post gave Schall direct access to the young Emperor, who was strongly influenced by the learning and the upright personality of this foreigner who had radically renounced all worldly pleasures. The Emperor respected Schall as a teacher and mentor, according him great trust and numerous signs of his favour. Schall received additional honorific offices and attained the highest rank of the official class. Thus he came to have considerable influence at court and with the Emperor himself, which he was able to use in many cases to advance the interests of the mission and of Christian teaching. But what was most important, in the bureaucratic structure of Chinese society, was the social prestige associated with his high and influential status in the headquarters of the government at the imperial court. No official in the capital or the provinces would have risked creating difficulties for himself and his adherents by provoking the adherents or friends of a man of such standing as Schall. Thus as long as Schall's fellow Jesuits did not cause an evident breach of public order, they were usually able to work as missionaries without any interference from the authorities and subordinate officials, on the strength of the respect in which Adam Schall's name was held. This, of course, provided only a temporary assurance of the status of the mission and was in no sense permanent and assured. Any change in the balance of power in Peking might mean difficulty or danger for the mission. This in fact took place at the death of the first Manchu Emperor in 1661. Schall's opponents immediately made use of this opportunity to take action against Schall and the other missionaries. He was accused on trumped up charges, deprived of his offices, imprisoned and condemned to death, but was finally pardoned. Shortly afterwards, in 1666, he died. The very moment Schall fell into disgrace at court, the mission lost its support elsewhere; this led to the persecution of the missionaries and their Chinese friends.

Soon, however, the situation changed once again in favour of the missionaries. As soon as the extremely able and energetic new Emperor came of age and set himself free from the guardianship of the regents, he saw through the plot that had been concocted against Schall, restored him posthumously to all his offices and honours, and in 1670, appointed a younger Jesuit, the Belgian Ferdinand Verbiest, known in Chinese as Nan Huai-Jen, as Schall's successor as the head of the Department of Astronomy. He followed this by appointing Verbiest to various honorific offices. Soon he came into close personal contact with the Emperor K'anghsi, who was one of the greatest rulers China has ever had. K'anghsi was well educated, possessed an exceedingly lucid understanding, and extensive scientific interests. Besides Verbiest, he gradually surrounded himself with other learned Jesuits, and loved to conduct long conversations with them, to be instructed by them in scientific questions of every kind, and to discuss them with him. The Emperor also entrusted special tasks to many of the Jesuit Fathers. Thus, for example, some of them acted as interpreters and advisers at the conclusion of the treaty of Nerchinsk between China and Russia, in 1689. Others played a decisive part in the preparation and publication of the great atlas of the Chinese Empire of 1717, known as the *Jesuit Map*.

Thus the K'anghsi period (1662–1722), the last great Golden Age of traditional China, was also a period when the Catholic mission flourished. The Jesuits were followed by Franciscan, Augustinian and Dominican missionaries, and also by secular priests of the Société des Missions Étrangères de Paris, founded in 1658. Well over one hundred foreign missionaries were active in every province of China (except Kansu and the border regions of Manchuria, Mongolia,

Sinkiang and Tibet), entirely thanks to the high status enjoyed by the learned and adaptable Jesuits at the imperial court in Peking. In 1663, the community in Peking alone numbered about 13,000 Christians. In the whole of China, at the beginning of the 18th century, there were well over 200,000 (something over 0.1 per cent of the whole population). By contrast to the early 17th century, when Ricci made it his main concern to win to Christianity members of the ruling bureaucratic class, at the beginning of the Manchu period the members of the Catholic communities were drawn more and more exclusively from the lower classes. Apart from a number of officials and staff of the Department of Astronomy, the Christian religion had only a few adherents in official circles. The later effect of this was to be extremely harmful.

4.   THE DECLINE OF THE MISSION AND ITS CAUSES

The activity of the mission had attained its highest point during the reign of K'anghsi, and a rapid decline followed. The propagation of Christian teaching was forbidden. Under K'anghsi, the prohibition was not strictly enforced, and only became fully effective under his successors. Most of the missionaries were expelled. Apart from a group in Peking, who worked at the Department of Astronomy or were employed elsewhere in different tasks by the Government, and had no political influence, only a few missionaries in the whole country were able to escape the increasing intensity of the persecution and remain in China. In spite of this, other new missionaries attempted to come to China. Many actually succeeded, and in some districts the number of adherents of Christianity in fact increased. After the beginning of the 18th century the total of Chinese Christians remained approximately the same— 200,000–300,000—without showing any significant increase. At the beginning of the 19th century there were only about thirty European missionaries in the whole of China, in addition to approximately 80 Chinese priests. After 1838 there were no longer any European missionaries in Peking, so that the tradition begun in 1601 by Ricci came to an end.

There were numerous reasons for the decline of the mission. They can be reduced to two basic factors. The first was an objective factor, and lay in the nature of Christianity on the one hand, and on the other in the social and religious circumstances of China. The second was subjective and resulted from the strategy and practice of the mission. The first objective factor can be broken down into a number of separate points.

1. The ruling bureaucratic class, the *Shen-shih*, possessed a privileged and leading position in the social structure, obtained by success in literary examinations. The *Shen-shih* were, moreover, the only class who possessed such a privileged position. Thus they were bound to resent the influence of a missionary or even of a member of the native clergy as a threat to their own exclusive and privileged position, if that influence were due to other qualities than success in the literary examination. If the Christian community in a village or a town became numerous, it was very easy for the head of this community to become more influential, and consequently more highly regarded, than the members of the *Shen-shih* class. Ricci, with his acute understanding of Chinese affairs, had made it his particular concern to win to Christianity members of the *Shen-shih* class. He sought as it were to integrate Christianity into the existing social order. A Christian *Shen-shih* had no cause in a largely Christian environment to be concerned for his privileged status; this might even be increased by his influence as the lay leader of the Christian community. This of course depended upon a certain discretion and adaptability on the part of a foreign missionary. Ricci possessed these qualities to an outstanding degree, and many other missionaries also displayed them. It was something that depended essentially upon the character of individual personalities. A number of other missionaries, however, were less discreet and adaptable, so that difficulties could easily arise. That at the time of Ricci and immediately afterwards, a number of *Shen-*

shih, including many of the best elements in this class, were converted to Christianity, is clearly shown by the comments of avowed opponents of Christianity. Those who were hostile to Christianity must have been filled with anxiety and anger by this fact. For if a member of the *Shen-shih* adopted Christianity this could easily result—especially in the country—in the whole neighbourhood becoming largely Christian. There is also evidence for this in the statements of opponents of Christianity.[1]

Relying on their position at the court of the Manchu Emperor, the missionaries seem as early as the beginning of the Ch'ing period to have been less concerned to gain new adherents within the *Shen-shih* class than Ricci and his direct successors. One reason for this may have been that at that time considerable numbers amongst the *Shen-shih*—including a number of the most eminent personalities of the day—adopted an outwardly reserved attitude to the foreign Manchu dynasty, and in their hearts rejected it. This lack of support among the *Shen-shih* had its effect as soon as the missionaries fell into disgrace at court, and were unable to find protection and refuge with influential Christian *Shen-shih* families in the provinces until the persecution was over, as they had done during the late Ming period.

This situation raises the question of how the Buddhist or Taoist priests were able to maintain their position in the structure of Chinese society. It would take too long to go into this matter in detail here. Buddhism had come to China at a period when the social order was far from being as fixed and stratified as it was a thousand years later. Thus it offered considerably less resistance to the spread of Buddhism than the later society did to the spread of Christianity. By the 16th century Buddhism in China had long since passed its peak. The social standing of Buddhist and Taoist priests at that time was usually rather low. Their services were customarily

[1] With the Chinese opinion of Christianity given here and in the pages that follow cf. Ch'en Yüan, 'Ts'ung chiao-wai tien-chi chien Ming-mo Ch'ing-ch'u chih t'ien-chu chiao', *Kuo-li Pei-p'ing t'u-shu-kuan kuan-k'an* 8, 1934, 2, pp. 1–31.

sought for burials and other ceremonies; people were prepared to pay them for this, and to provide for their livelihood in other ways, but not to pay any serious regard to them. Thus as soon as Ricci had recognised the position, he separated himself completely from Buddhist and Taoists, since their social position did not seem to him to be one worth seeking.

2. In spite of the opposition to it, Buddhism gained acceptance in many educated circles in China. The reason for the opposition was that Buddhist teaching contradicted many Chinese and especially Confucian customs and views. No questions of external politics were involved. This was not the case with Christianity. From the middle of the 15th century on the Ming Empire had constantly been threatened by external enemies; in the north by the Mongols and later by the Manchus, and in the coastal regions, from Kuangtung right up to Korea, by the Japanese. Similarly, during the first decades of Manchu rule there were constant conflicts with the survivors of the Ming dynasty, and with the Mongols and other border peoples. Thus there was a distrust of all foreigners, and an inclination to see in them foreign agents and spies. Ricci gives a very clear description of this experience on the occasion of the Japanese invasion of Korea in 1598.[1] Over and above this, the foreign missionaries possessed outstanding technical ability and were able to manufacture various mechanical devices. They even constructed cannon both for the Ming against the Manchu and later for the Manchu themselves. This increased the mistrust of them on the part of the Chinese, as can be seen from numerous statements by well-known Chinese personalities of that period.

The Chinese often found it difficult to believe that the foreign missionaries had only come to China from an idealistic desire to spread their religion, without any other aim. Other intentions were often suspected, and attempts were made to discover them. Even Ricci constantly encountered this

[1] Louis J. Gallagher, *China in the Sixteenth Century: The Journals of Matthew Ricci 1583–1610*, Toronto 1953, pp. 299–300.

suspicion, as can be seen for example from the last sentence of the letter of Li Cho-wu (Ch. IV, §1 above).

3. In China religious sects were often associated with movements of revolt, due to social causes, on the part of oppressed and economically deprived classes. It was easy for such movements to spread rapidly over a wide area. Sometimes they presented a serious threat to the government of the day, and in some cases had been known to bring about the downfall of the ruling dynasty. Thus the Chinese authorities were suspicious of every new religious tendency, especially if it was particularly evident amongst the lower classes. It was inevitable that Christianity should become the object of such suspicion. Ricci was conscious of this danger. He tried to counter it by extensive assimilation to the manner of life and thought of Confucianism, which reflected the existing social order, and by associating the mission with the ruling Confucian *Shen-shih* class. He also emphatically opposed Buddhism, Taoism and the popular religion. Nevertheless he was unable to avert all suspicion from himself, and this was even more the case with his less adaptable successors.

Time and again, after the arrest of foreign missionaries or native Christians, the authorities carrying out the investigation had to make the astonished admission that they were orderly and peaceful people who obeyed the laws, and did nothing that was forbidden. This can be seen from numerous documents from the 18th century, when Christianity was officially forbidden. The question has since been asked, whether the interests of the mission might perhaps have been better served if it had identified itself less with orthodox Confucianism, and associated itself with the circles which were critical of this orthodoxy. In the late 16th century, such unorthodox movements were of considerable importance amongst the disciples and adherents of Wang Yang-ming. One of the best known advocates of such views was Li Cho-wu, the acquaintance of Ricci mentioned above, who was later tried for the publication of heretical works, and who died in prison in 1602. When we look back, it seems extremely doubtful whether Christianity would have achieved a better response in these unorthodox circles—Li Cho-wu's statement concerning Ricci makes this very unlikely—and it is most improbable that in union with the heretical groups, it could have become sufficiently strong to prevail against Confucian orthodoxy. This suggests that in the circumstances of the time the missionary strategy of Ricci was the best. Confucian orthodoxy was too firmly rooted, and only upheavals as violent as those which occurred after the middle of the 19th century were able to overthrow this orthodoxy and with it the traditional Chinese political and social system.

4. Certain traditional Chinese customs and ways of thought were opposed to Christian teaching. It would take too long here to go into this in detail, but it would be an interesting task. In particular, the thinking of the educated class, formed by Confucianism, was agnostic and unfavourable to all metaphysics, and concentrated on this world and its problems, and consequently made difficult the spread of a religious doctrine largely oriented towards the next world. As a result of its metaphysical element, therefore, Christianity was frequently regarded by members of the educated class as being on the same level as the highly superstitious Buddhist and Taoist popular religion. But that in spite of these difficulties a number of prominent members of the educated class found it possible to accept Christianity, is explained by the particular readiness of the 16th and 17th century in China to accept new ideas, and by the intellectual curiosity of many educated persons. The Emperor K'anghsi himself was one of these. The outstanding scientific knowledge and intellectual ability of the learned missionaries attracted many educated Chinese. Thus it became possible for the Jesuit fathers also to influence these educated persons in a religious direction, and to lead many of them to accept Christianity.

The importance of the personality of an individual missionary must not be under-estimated. For the Chinese often tend to regard one's personality as being of greater importance than the view one represents. What is willingly accorded to

someone whom they find attractive can equally emphatically
be refused to another who is unable to make such an impression.
Thus many Chinese may have become Christians out of
veneration and love for the person of Ricci rather than from
conviction of the truth of Christian teaching. Neither at the
time of Ricci, nor later, did those who directed the mission
often show themselves aware of this Chinese characteristic.

It also seems that in spite of the adoption of the Christian
religion by educated Chinese, their traditional Confucian
outlook remained predominant. This conclusion is apparently forced on us by the following facts. Ch'ü Shih-szu, the
principal minister of the Emperor Yungli of the Southern
Ming Dynasty (cf. Ch. IV, §2), who was a Christian, voluntarily
allowed himself to be taken prisoner by the enemy troops
when he realised that the position of his imperial master was
hopeless. As a loyal subject of the Ming Dynasty, he rejected
offers of a place in the service of the Manchu, and was condemned to death. Several weeks passed before his execution.
It was still hoped to win him over to the service of the Manchu.
During this period Ch'ü Shih-szu composed a number of
poems which have been preserved. One would have expected
that Ch'ü would have found comfort and strength in his
Christian faith in the face of imminent death, and that in some
way these poems would have reflected the Christian attitude
of their author towards life and death. Instead, the poems
are written exclusively in a traditional Confucian spirit, and
contain not the slightest hint of any Christian thought. The
poems could just as well have been written by a Chinese who
had never in his life heard anything of Christianity. One cannot
but conclude that the Christian faith did not go very deep in the
case of many educated Chinese.

A number of Confucian customs and practices concerning
which there was some doubt as to whether they were com-
patible with Christian teaching—as for example the cult of
Confucius or the veneration of ancestors—were expressly
tolerated by the Jesuits. On the other hand, there were other
customs which could in no case be reconciled with Christianity,

as for example polygamy, which for the Chinese was not only permissible, but could actually become a moral duty if the first wife produced no children or no son, so that the head of the house was not in a position to fulfil his duty of continuing the male line of his family. This very question in fact often dissuaded people from receiving Christian baptism, although every other condition was fulfilled. Although even in this case, a number of far-sighted and broad-minded Jesuit Fathers must have turned a blind eye in the interest of the mission as a whole, there could in theory be no compromise in this matter.

The highest aim of the Jesuit missionaries was the conversion of the Chinese Emperor to Christianity. In the case of the last Ming Emperor, as also in the case of the two first Manchu rulers, Shunchih and K'anghsi, the Jesuits, or some of them at least, regard this goal as being within reach. These hopes were most strongly expressed by Jesuits writing in Europe far from the realities of China, and there can scarcely have been any ground for them in spite of all the achievements of individual fathers such as Adam Schall or Ferdinand Verbiest. In China the dualism between state and church, between the secular and spiritual power, did not exist as it did in Europe. The position of the Chinese Emperor was that of a *pontifex maximus* in a universal secular-ecclesiastical state, of the type described by Max Weber as Caesaro-papist. It was of no importance in this context that the original basis of this secular-ecclesiastical state had become extensively secularised in the course of time, and contained very few metaphysical elements. As the Son of Heaven and as the representative of Heaven the Emperor possessed an exclusive position which was simply irreconcilable with subjection to a foreign ecclesiastical organisation and its head. The conversion of the Chinese Emperor to a foreign religion would have seemed almost as monstrous as if the Pope had become a Mohammedan and still remained head of the Catholic Church. A fundamental change in the traditional structure of the Chinese state and Chinese society would have been necessary before its head could have accepted a foreign religion. Thus a limit was imposed here on the spread of Christianity. The personal interest taken by the first two Manchu Emperors in the missionaries was due in the first place to their scientific knowledge. To this must be added, in some cases, a particular regard for the compelling personalities of individual missionaries. This regard was paid to the person of the missionary himself, but not to the religion he represented.

The points mentioned so far were objectively hindrances to the spread of Christianity in China, which lay in the nature of the situation. We have shown how Ricci and other Jesuits to some extent recognised the difficulties for what they were, and sought to counter them. By a far-seeing missionary strategy they were able to avoid and neutralise the difficulties in part, but not to remove them. Every mistake and every thoughtless action on the part of a missionary caused difficulties that had been overcome to return with renewed force. Thus even if Ricci's missionary strategy had been carried on with a full consciousness of its aims and with the utmost skill, it is extremely doubtful whether the desired goal would have been attained and a significant percentage of the Chinese population led to Christianity. But it is undoubtedly true that the way laid down by Ricci, the extensive adaptation of Christianity to the Chinese situation, was the only one which offered any chance of giving to Christianity any greater significance in China than that of a popular religious sect. We come here to the subjective causes for the decline of the mission, to be found in the attitude of the Church and its representatives. They can all be reduced to a single point, known as the controversy over Chinese rites.

Ricci's missionary strategy of the extensive adaptation of Christianity to the circumstances of China, and especially the toleration of Confucian rites, such as the cult of Confucius, the veneration of the Emperor and of one's own ancestors, etc., did not remain unchallenged either within his own order or outside. But it was able to prevail within the Jesuit mission, which as a result possessed by far the strongest influence amongst the various missionary societies in China. The other societies only accepted in part the practice of the Jesuits. As a result of a campaign beginning in the second half of the 17th century, and instigated in particular by the Jansenists against the Jesuit Order as such, the opposition to their missionary practice visibly ceased to be objective in character. The criticism and condemnation of the missionary practice instituted by Ricci became increasingly nothing more than a weapon in the hands of the enemies of the Jesuit Order in Europe, who neither understood anything of the circumstances in China, nor possessed any understanding or interest in the Chinese mission as such. Their principal aim was to reduce the influence of the Jesuits. Even before the final dissolution of the Jesuit order, the Papal Bull *Ex illa die* of 1715 definitely condemned the missionary practice of the Jesuits, forbade the toleration of Chinese rites and insisted on the practice of Christianity in China in its European form. Western nationalism and colonialism, which were coming powerfully to the fore at that period, and the feeling of superiority over the non-European peoples associated with them, led also to an increasing contempt for the Chinese and their civilisation. Even amongst the Jesuits who sought to preserve the tradition of Ricci, the concern for a thorough study of the Chinese language and literature, and for a fundamental and sympathetic understanding of Chinese civilisation, gradually decreased. Thus by 1720 the Emperor had to admit that none of the missionaries who were at work at the imperial court was any longer able to speak good Chinese.

The prohibition of Chinese rites meant that Chinese Christians were prevented from exercising their civil duties. According to the Chinese view, this meant that doubt was cast on the loyalty of Chinese Christians to the state and to society. An interpretation of the Chinese rites by the Roman curia which differed from the official Chinese interpretation—identical with that of the Jesuits—and the demand that the Chinese should recognise the Roman understanding of them, was found to be regarded by the Chinese as an intolerable interference in Chinese affairs. The Chinese government could

E

not fail to react. Even during the reign of K'anghsi, who was broad-minded and altogether favourably inclined towards the Jesuits, the propagation of Christian teaching was forbidden throughout China.

Further discredit was brought on Christianity by the unworthy form which the conflict concerning Chinese rites sometimes took between the orders at work in the mission and between individual personalities. Its final culmination was the delivery in Peking of the decree dissolving the Society of Jesus, in the year 1774, in most degrading circumstances. Similarly, the arrogant behaviour of individual Roman envoys to the imperial court strengthened the existing aversion and mistrust on the part of the Chinese. It is true that in spite of prohibition and persecution, many Chinese Christians remained faithful to their religion. But they were limited more and more to the lower classes, so that the Chinese came to regard Christianity as equivalent to the popular Taoist and Buddhist sects. An attitude of contempt was added to their mistrust of a foreign doctrine. This developed to the extent that members of the *Shen-shih* class, whose ancestors had been Christians at the end of the Ming period, zealously revoked all traces of this fact in their own writings or in those of others. For such a connection with Christianity was regarded as a great shame upon the family. Thus Christianity in China had been reduced to the exact situation which Ricci sought to avoid at all costs. Later, of course—albeit 260 years too late to alter the course of events—Ricci and the other Jesuits were acknowledged to be right. In 1939 their point of view in the matter of Chinese rites was officially sanctioned by the Roman *Curia* and their practice completely rehabilitated.

The opinion has recently been expressed that in the ominous decisions made by Rome in the question of Chinese rites at the end of the 17th and the beginning of the 18th centuries, the basis was laid for the unfortunate course taken by the encounter between China and the West in the 19th and 20th centuries. With the Communist take-over of 1948–49, this encounter reached a new stage in its development. There is much, in fact, to be said for this view. What course might the development of the relationship between China and the West have taken if the mission had consistently followed the direction laid down by Ricci? Perhaps a strong indigenous Christianity, firmly rooted in China and thoroughly Chinese in its ways, might have formed a bridge to assist China and the West to understand each other. In the second half of the 19th century, the mission might perhaps have been sufficiently strong to renounce a close association with the colonial Powers and their imperialist intentions, and to work instead for mutual understanding and agreement. And it might also have been possible for Christianity to have played a decisive part in the transformation of the traditional China into a modern society. Such speculations are not without their attraction. But they seem at the present day rather too unreal and hypo-thetical. The decision taken in the controversy over Chinese rites may perhaps have been, as we have suggested, only one symptom of the europocentric attitude, conditioned by nation-alism and colonialist imperialism, and one symptom of the European hubris, which it is so enormously difficult nowadays for us completely to overcome. From this point of view, the decision taken in the controversy over Chinese rites was only the beginning of an imperialist missionary strategy which was consistently pursued throughout the 19th and early 20th centuries. The mission simply became one expression of the intellectual attitude of that period. Those who represented it were children of their time, and apart from the few exceptions who only confirmed the rule, were unable to break away from the conceptions of the world in which they had grown up and in which they lived.

5. THE EFFECT OF THE INCREASED KNOWLEDGE OF CHINA IN EUROPE

So far we have only spoken of one aspect of the Christian mission, and of the Jesuit mission in particular, that is, its activities in China and its effect upon China. The effect of the mission upon European intellectual life was equally great, and perhaps even more important. As we have already shown (§1 above) the description of China given by a small number of Portuguese and Spanish writers gave Europe vital new knowledge of China. This new knowledge far exceeded what had been learned from Marco Polo. A book on China by the Spanish Augustinian Juan Gonzalez de Mendoza, first published in 1585, and based upon these accounts, was gradually translated into all European languages and read by almost all educated Europeans. An English translation of the work was published in 1588 with the title: *The Historie of the great and mightie kingdome of China, and the situation thereof: Togither with the great riches, huge Citties, politike gouernement and rare inuentions in the same.* Mendoza recounted much that was new concerning the customs, usages, society and civilisation of China, about which Marco Polo had had little to say. This work provided the first basis on which a new picture of China could be built up in the West. For over a century after this, this picture of China was largely shaped by the descriptions of the Jesuits. It has already been noted that Ricci was the true discoverer of Chinese intellectual culture. His accounts were first published in Latin in 1615 by his fellow Jesuit Trigault, and soon afterwards appeared in other European languages. Like Mendoza's book, Ricci's came to be one of the most popular books of the time. Further general studies of China followed, and were also translated into various languages. Amongst the best known are those of Fr. Athanasius Kircher (1667), Fr. Louis le Comte (1696) and the work of Fr. du Halde, *Description géographique, historique, chronologique, politique et physique de l'empire de la Chine et de la Tartarie chinoise* (1735), which is still used today. Fr. du Halde also published the descriptions given in the correspondence of the Peking Jesuits, which since 1702 have generally been known by the title *Lettres édifiantes et curieuses écrites des missions étrangères par quelques missionaires de la Compagnie de Jésus.* An English edition was published after 1707 with the title *Edifying and Curious*

Letters of some Missioners, of the Society of Jesus, from Foreign Missions.

In 1662 the Jesuits published in Peking the first translations of part of the Confucian Canonical Writings, in Latin.

This new knowledge of China produced a powerful impression in the West. Its effect was very far reaching; in particular, the newly discovered intellectual world of China came as a revelation to the European academic world. It was the French Jesuits who had played the largest part in the China mission, and their reports fell on particularly fruitful ground in France. The chronology of the early history of China and its relationship to the Old Testament tradition at once aroused great interest. The religious and philosophical questions raised, however, were of more vital significance. Eminent thinkers such as Pierre Bayle (1647–1706), Malebranche (1638–1715), Fénelon (1651–1715), Montesquieu (1689–1755), Voltaire (1694–1778) and others were considerably influenced by China in some of their ideas. Thus for example the Enlightenment claimed to recognise the ideals they were seeking in what they called 'the practical philosophy' of the Chinese and in the social and political systems based upon it. Voltaire considered that in China the theory of a universal religion of reason existed in reality. His admiration for China was expressed in words such as these:

> One does not have to be an enthusiast for the achievements of the Chinese to recognise that the constitution of their Empire is the most excellent the world has ever seen, and the only one based on patriarchal authority.[1]

Those who were called physiocrats, and particularly the originator of the physiocratic doctrine François Quesney (1694–1774), also came under the influence of the Chinese economic system, in which the possession of land and agriculture had always played a decisive role.

In Germany, the influence of the Jesuits' descriptions of

[1] *Oeuvres complètes*, Gotha 1785, XXXVIII, 492; quoted from A. Reichwein, *China and Europe*, New York 1925.

China is most notably evident in Leibniz's (1646–1716) and Christian Wolff's (1679–1754) works. Leibniz's *Novissima Sinica historiam nostri temporis illustratura*, which appeared in 1697, displays the utmost enthusiasm for China. In one passage he writes:

> Our circumstances seem to me to have sunk to such a level, particularly with regard to the monstrous and increasing breakdown of morality, that one could almost think it necessary for the Chinese to send missionaries to us to teach us the purpose and use of natural theology, in the same way as we send missionaries to them to instruct them in revealed theology. And I believe that if a wise man were set up to judge not the beauty of goddesses but the excellence of nations, we would give the golden apple to the Chinese, were it not that we excel them in one single but superhuman quality, the divine gift of the Christian religion.[1]

The ideal of the peaceful 'great harmony' which Leibniz sought to see in Europe, and which was so far from being realised, is closely related to the Chinese idea of the *ta t'ung*, the 'great unity' or 'one world', or however this expression is to be translated.

Though Leibniz may have held too idealised a view of China, in one fundamental insight he was centuries ahead of his time. The statements we have quoted, and other similar comments by Leibniz and many of his contemporaries, were the first to foreshadow a truly universal understanding of human civilisation. Leibniz came particularly close to seeing the wholly relative significance of Western civilisation in its proper light when he wrote:

> It is in my view a unique disposition of fate which has placed the highest civilisations the human race has achieved as it were at the two extremities of our continent, that is in Europe and in China, which adorns the opposite end of the earth as a kind of oriental Europe. And the highest providence is also at work in the fortunate circumstance that while the nations which are most highly developed and at the same time the furthest separated,

---

[1] Quoted from Otto Franke 'Leibniz und China', *Zeitschrift der Deutschen Morgenländischen Gesellschaft*, N.F. 7, 1928, pp. 155–178 (this quotation from p. 165).

reach out their arms to one another, everything that lies between them is gradually brought to a higher way of life.[1]

Leibniz clearly recognised that along with Western civilisation, that of China or of Eastern Asia, the common basis of which is the civilisation of China, is of the greatest significance for the whole world. This insight on the part of Leibniz is even today far from being generally understood in the West.

The influence of China on Christian Wolff became widely known as a result of a university lecture in Halle in 1721, on the theme *De Sinarum philosophia practica*. In this, he praised the morality of Confucius and placed it on the same level as Christian morality. Such utterances scandalised the Protestant theologians in Halle, who were far less broad-minded than the Catholic Jesuits. Wolff was accused of atheism and had to leave Halle and Prussia for a short time. He was received at the University of Marburg, until Frederick the Great called him back to Prussia.

The picture of China given by the Jesuits was that of a great and powerful empire enjoying peace, quiet and prosperity. At its head stood a wise and civilised ruler who ruled according to the precepts of reason and of a noble political ethic. The people were guided by the laws of a lofty and pure morality. Arts and sciences flourished and were held in equal honour by all classes. Life flowed on in a system governed by fixed and established forms. All war and conflict was outlawed, and the greatest commandment was that of peace and harmony. By contrast with this, Europe, divided and ravaged by constant war, and reduced to poverty and wretchedness after the Thirty Years War, presented a lamentable picture.

It is in fact true that in the 17th and early 18th centuries, the traditional China was enjoying the last Golden Age of its political and cultural life, and conditions there were in many respects far better than in Europe. Nevertheless, the picture of China painted by the Jesuits was far too idealistic. There is, of course, a particular reason for this. The controversy

[1] Ibid. pp. 173–174.

concerning Chinese rites was beginning, and in order to improve their position in this controversy the Jesuits in Paris tried to put across as ideal a view as possible of China and the Chinese. The letters and reports sent home by the Jesuit Fathers in China, which were entirely realistic and described the circumstances that actually existed, were very carefully edited before they were published in Paris. Any observations which were derogatory to the Chinese, or which were not easy to reconcile with Christianity, were eliminated. Fr. du Halde was particularly involved in this editing, and carried it out very thoroughly. This is the only possible reason why China could be regarded at that time by many—such as Leibniz— as a better world altogether, and in fact as almost a *civitas Dei*.

But in the late 17th and early 18th centuries, China, with its practical philosophy, became a dominant theme not merely in philosophical and political discussions. China also played a decisive role in art, and above all in the whole elegant and polished way of life represented by Rococo style. Chinese porcelain, lacquered work, painted and printed silks, wallpapers and many other articles were much sought after in Europe at that time. They were produced in China especially for export and brought in great quantities to Europe, where to an increasing extent they were successfully imitated. Chinese motifs were used in architecture, in landcape gardening and in ornaments of every kind. They dominated the whole of the elegant life of that period. In the process, however, they became more and more debased into an exotic and bizarre *chinoiserie*, which no longer had anything in common with what was genuinely Chinese.

As time went on, the idealised accounts of China given by the Jesuits were followed by an increasing number of descriptions produced by merchants. As a rule, the merchants had little interest in Chinese civilisation and Chinese intellectual life. Their accounts tended to the opposite extreme to those of the Jesuits, and are frequently characterised by spiteful, contemptuous and disdainful descriptions of the Chinese. Those who composed them were concerned exclusively with trade and profit; they came into contact in China only with the lower classes in the sea-ports and with subordinate officials who did not always belong to the best elements of the nation. In Europe the cosmopolitan and broad-minded approach of someone like Leibniz gave way to an outlook exclusively concentrated upon Europe. The renaissance of Greek and Roman antiquity in European intellectual life, the development of natural science and technology, the colonial expansion based on superior technological and military skill, and an attitude of mind devoted to power and profit, all played their part in creating an outlook centred entirely upon Europe. The derogatory accounts of China which were becoming available flattered the vanity and self-complacency of Europe. There was no longer any obvious reason for a serious concern with China. China ultimately became the object of grotesque caricature and ridicule. The window opened upon China by Ricci and his successors was closed again at the end of the 18th and the beginning of the 19th centuries. Europe and China knew of each other's existence, but neither desired to know the other better, let alone to understand each other. Aversion and contempt characterised the attitude each held towards the other. This boded ill for the future.

V

The Colonial Invasion of China

1. THE ADVANCE OF THE COLONIAL POWERS IN CHINA

The first period of direct association by sea between China and and West ended in 1644 with the fall of the Ming Dynasty. From the very first these direct links between China and the West had been unfortunate. Ignorance of each other's intellectual and cultural background, resulting in mutual misunderstandings, already characterised the Chinese attitude to the Portuguese, and henceforth formed a decisive element in the relationship between China and the West right down to the present day.

As early as the 17th century the leading rôle played by the Portuguese in trade with China was challenged by the Dutch. Soon, however, Britain established an increasingly dominant position as the chief Western commercial Power and as the champion of Western interests in China. In the first forty years after the establishment of Manchu rule, the situation in China, which had not yet been stabilised after the change of dynasty, in fact reduced foreign maritime trade to a minimum. Only after 1685 were British and other European merchants gradually able to build up their trade in the ports of Canton, Amoy, Fuchou and Ningpo; in the case of the last three ports, however, this was only a temporary development, for in 1760 all foreign trade was concentrated at Canton at the wish of the Chinese government. As a result Canton soon developed into an important and flourishing commercial metropolis.

Like every other association with China on the part of Europeans, trade was conducted at that period according to the conditions laid down by China, on the pattern which China fixed for both parties to observe. In 1685 the Chinese government appointed an official to superintend foreign trade and the collection of customs duties in Canton. He came to be known in the West by the title Hoppo, according to one explanation from the *hupu*, the Finance Ministry, to which he had to hand over the dues he collected. The office of the Hoppo goes back to similar institutions set up to regulate foreign trade with the Arabs and Persians from the 8th century A.D. on. In accordance with Chinese tradition, the Chinese government did not leave maritime trade to the free initiative of private merchants, but claimed the monopoly itself. The government, however, did not exercise this monopoly, but assigned it to a number of Chinese merchants, who traded with the foreigners as agents of the government. In Western writings this group of merchants is known as the Cohong. The foreign merchants were only allowed to live in 'factories' placed in narrowly restricted areas outside the walls of Canton, and were not permitted to enter the city. Only the Hong merchants were allowed to deal directly with the foreigners, and to a certain degree were even made responsible by the Chinese authorities for the behaviour of the foreigners.

On the British side, the East India Company possessed a monopoly of the China trade up to 1834. After that date it was possible for all British merchants to trade with China. To supervise the trade and to take care of the interests of the British merchants, the British government sent a plenipotentiary to Canton. Whereas previously no more than a few persons or groups representing particular interests from Europe had ever established any connection with the Chinese, there was now for the first time—apart from a small number of envoys sent on particular missions—a permanent official representative of a Western government in China. For the first time, China was directly confronted with a Western state as such. The official representative of the powerful British Empire did not consider himself able to tolerate the Chinese claim to have superior jurisdiction, and the treatment meted out to the British by China as a result of this claim. Disputes between the two sides increased. They were due in part to objective reasons, and notably to the fundamentally different view of relationships between states held by the Chinese and the British (cf. Ch. III, §2 above). A characteristic example of this is the following occurrence. In the year 1839, at the beginning of the Opium dispute, a letter from the British to the Chinese Governor-General in Canton spoke of 'the maintenance of peace between the two countries' (i.e. between China and Britain). In the answer given by the Governor-General the following words occur:

> . . . In regard to the style of the address, there is much that cannot be understood. Thus, for instance, the words "the two countries", I know not the meaning of. While our Celestial Court has in humble submission to it ten thousand (i.e. all) regions, and the heaven-like goodness of the great Emperor overshadows all, the nations aforesaid and the Americans have, by their trade at Canton during many years, enjoyed, of all those in subjection, the largest measure of favours. And I presume, it must be England and America, that are conjointly named "the two countries". But the meaning of the language is greatly wanting in perspicuity.[1]

In addition to this fundamental difference of outlook there were subjective causes of misunderstanding due to human inadequacy on both sides. The question of the import of opium was a powerful source of conflict. It had developed into a lucrative business for both British and Chinese traders. For the administration of British India the export of opium had become a financial necessity, and consequently, in spite of many critical voices at home, the British government gave a free hand to the opium merchants. The Chinese government attempted to oppose the import of this dangerous narcotic, and the associated outflow of Chinese silver. The conflict was extended by the interest certain Chinese circles had in the opium trade, and by the dispute as to the share of profits to be taken by the various parties involved.

The intensifying conflict between the Chinese and the British finally led in 1840 to what is known as the Opium War,

---

[1] Quoted from the English translation by J. Robert Morrison in *Correspondence Relating to China, Blue Books*, 36, 1840, p. 369. The Chinese original is unfortunately not known.

the first decisive military encounter between China and the West. In this war the superiority of Western weapons and Western tactics became obvious. The Peace of Nanking, which ended the war in 1842, provided that Hong Kong should be ceded to Britain and that Canton, Amoy, Fuchou, Ningpo and Shanghai should be opened to foreign trade as 'treaty ports'. The treaty of Nanking was the first of what are known as the 'unequal treaties', which laid down the pattern for those that followed, and it led in the course of the next few decades to increasingly ignominious humiliations of China. In addition to the treaty with Britain the years that followed brought similar treaties with the United States, France, Belgium, Sweden, Norway and Portugal, and later also with Russia and Prussia. The Chinese showed themselves very half-hearted in carrying out the concessions they had been forced to make. They hoped, as before, that some day they would be rid of the foreigners. The obvious military weakness of China by comparison with the Western Powers encouraged the latter to behave in an increasingly aggressive way, so that fresh conflicts occurred. Britain and France used—and perhaps intentionally provoked—insignificant squabbles as an excuse for fresh military interventions, in order to obtain fresh advantages and profits. In the Treaty of Tientsin of 1858 China was forced by a French and British military expedition to make fresh concessions. Two years later British and French troops advanced as far as Peking. The sacking and total destruction of the great imperial palace outside Peking (*Yüanmingyüan*) by the British troops could only serve to confirm the Chinese view that the Europeans were nothing more than a new category of uncivilised barbarians.

Up to the 1860s the aims of the foreign Powers consisted principally in the profitable extension of their trade. In the period that followed they no longer restricted themselves to this policy, but sought to establish positions of strength in a strategy of power politics, and to enjoy unrestricted opportunities of economic expansion; in short they were trying to extend their colonial empire. The Great Powers of the West were joined by Japan, which had rapidly increased its political and economic strength. In the 1870s the Russians occupied the Ili region of Central Asia, and the Japanese took the Liukiu Islands in 1880; in 1885 France forced China to cede Annam (Vietnam), which had been under Chinese suzerainty, and in 1886 Burma, which was also a Chinese tribute state, was ceded to Britain. Formosa and the Pescadores were ceded to Japan as a result of China's defeat in the war of 1894–95, and Korea was declared to be independent of Chinese suzerainty, and was ultimately annexed by Japan. In 1897 Germany occupied Tsingtao and the Gulf of Kiaochou on a trivial pretext, and in the years that followed Russia occupied Port Arthur and Dairen, France Kuangchouwan and Britain Weihaiwei. Extensive economic concessions covering mining, the construction of railways, etc., in every part of China had already been obtained. In addition, individual Powers had obtained provisions by treaty ensuring that large areas of China would not be ceded to other Powers. This implied the area mentioned would be an exclusive sphere of influence for the country in question, and was earmarked for later annexation as a colony. Thus Central China around the Yangtse valley was reckoned as a British sphere of influence, and the South and South-West as that of the French. Fukien was reserved to the Japanese. The Russian sphere of influence included the whole of Manchuria and extended to Chihli (Hopei) province. The Germans were firmly established in Shantung. It was already customary at that time to speak of 'German China' in the same way as of 'German East Africa'. Thus at the end of the 19th century China seemed close to being divided amongst foreign Powers in the same way as Africa. But the mutual jealousy of the imperialist Powers played an important part in preventing such a development. The Boxer Rising of 1900 was the last confused attempt of the old China to drive out the foreign intruders by force. It was paid for by fresh humiliations.

2. THE 'UNEQUAL TREATIES'

Up to the beginning of the Opium War Western merchants had largely accepted the conditions of trade laid down by China, and the tribute system (cf. Ch. III, §2 above) had also provided an institutional framework for the relationship of the Chinese to the Europeans. With the Treaty of Nanking this framework was broken into for the first time, and a new institutional basis set up for relations between the states concerned. The Treaty of Nanking and the treaties that immediately followed were still, however, the result of a compromise between the traditional Chinese view and Western conceptions of dealings between one state and another. But they progressively became the expression of Western dominance in China, and for this reason were later known by the Chinese as 'unequal treaties'. The characteristic features of these 'unequal treaties' can be summed up in four essential points, which imposed severe restrictions on Chinese sovereignty:

1. The extraterritoriality of foreigners in China, in association with consular jurisdiction. On the basis of the Western idea of the territoriality of law, the British hesitated at first, after the conclusion of the Opium War, to make what was by Western standards an exceedingly far-reaching claim. But it was granted by China without any particular misgivings and was laid down for the first time in the agreement of 1843 which supplemented the Treaty of Nanking (Art. IX). For according to the dominant view in China, a person is always covered by the law of his native country wherever he resides. A thousand years previously, 'barbarians' trading in China had been permitted without question, and even in fact expected, to decide their own cases themselves according to their own law (cf. Ch. III, §4 above). Only later, when the Chinese view itself changed, and the disadvantages of such an arrangement for China began to be felt, were the extraterritoriality of foreigners and consular jurisdiction regarded as a serious intrusion upon Chinese sovereignty. Right up to the second World War the Great Powers of the West obstinately maintained this privilege.

2. The restriction of the level of customs duties. From 1858 on import and export duties were levied at a single fixed percentage for all goods. From 1854 the administration of maritime customs duties had been carried out by foreigners, even though the Inspector-General, who was always an Englishman, and the other foreign inspectors were officially subordinate to Chinese officials and therefore to the Chinese Emperor. It was also true that this branch of the administration was incorrupt and trustworthy, by contrast with almost every other department in China at the time (cf. §4 below). The treaties also provided that once a duty had been exacted upon foreign goods they could not be subject to any internal tax, unlike home-produced goods. The restriction of the level of customs duties placed a powerful brake upon the development of the Chinese economy, and prevented the building up of China's own industry, which would have been possible at first only with the aid of certain protective tariffs.

3. Foreign settlements, concessions and leased territories. In many of the ports open to foreign trade the treaties had provided that the foreigners should have particular residential areas for their exclusive use, and these, although *de jure* they remained Chinese territory, were under foreign administration and were policed by the foreigners, and lay outside the jurisdiction of the Chinese authorities. A distinction was made between international settlements such as existed in Shanghai, Amoy, Chefoo, Fuchou or Tsinan, and concessions which were granted to a particular nation, such as the French concession in Shanghai, the British, French, Japanese, Russian, Italian, Belgian, and Austrian concessions in Tientsin etc. The foreign Powers possessed the right to station troops in the international settlements and in the concessions, and were later allowed to have troops in Peking to protect their legations. The territories that were leased, such as the 'new territories' of Kowloon (opposite Hong Kong), Tsingtao, Kuangchouwan, etc., were usually leased to the foreigners for 99 years.

4. Freedom of movement for foreign ships in Chinese inland and territorial waters.

In addition to all this there was also the notorious 'most favoured nation clause', which from the time of the Anglo-Chinese supplementary agreement of 1843 was included in almost every treaty. It stipulated that all the rights which the Chinese should ever concede to other nations in the future would automatically be accorded to the signatory of the treaty. Through this clause, the United States and other European countries profited from the privileges which Britain and France had obtained, in part by force of arms. At first the Chinese raised no objection to this clause, for it corresponded to the traditional idea that all barbarians should share equally in the favour of the Chinese Emperor (cf. Ch. III, §4 above). It was not until later that the real force of this stipulation was realised; it deprived China of a considerable part of her freedom of political action, particularly with regard to trading policy.

As we have already mentioned, the provisions in the treaties which placed notable limitations on Chinese sovereignty were not felt by China at first to be excessively onerous. It was true that they were regarded as very troublesome concessions which had had to be made under pressure; but they did not directly affect the fundamental basis of China's political structure with regard to foreign nations, and in theory made possible the continuance of the traditional tribute system. What was decisive for the Chinese was the according of fundamentally equal rights both to foreign nations and to China. Up to the time of the Opium War the representatives of Western nations who occasionally came to the Chinese capital had either to follow the traditional Chinese ceremonial or go away without an audience with the Emperor (cf. Ch. III, §2 above). The Treaty of Nanking left the question of diplomatic representation open. Not until the negotiations which took place in Tientsin in 1858 to end the armed conflict with Britain and France, did the British insist on provision for this. They required that the documents ratifying the treaty should be exchanged in Peking, and that Britain should receive the right to establish a permanent diplomatic mission in the Chinese capital. The French, Russian and Americans associated them-

F

selves with the British demand, although they were less insistent. When they were negotiating treaties, the Chinese were ready to make concessions in numerous other directions, and their thinking at that time, which was wholly in accordance with their traditional practice, made it impossible for them to anticipate the oppressive limitation of Chinese sovereignty which these concessions would later cause. By contrast, the British demand to establish a permanent ambassador in Peking who would represent there the British Queen—a woman!— as a sovereign possessing equal rights with the Chinese Emperor, was irreconcilable with the dignity of the Chinese ruling house. Nevertheless, the British plenipotentiary conducting the negotiations, having regard to the further development of relations between Britain and China, regarded this condition as indispensable. He even considered himself justified in forcing its inclusion in the treaty (Art. II–V) by the threat of armed intervention. After signing the treaty, the Chinese representatives were most severely reproached by the Emperor, and instructed to revoke this article completely in the negotiations which followed concerning the carrying out of the treaty. The British plenipotentiary himself then declared that he was willing not to insist on the fulfilment of this part of the treaty for the time being. But the Chinese government was not content with this modification. The question of the exchange of the documents of ratification in Peking led to a renewed outbreak of hostilities, which resulted in 1860 in the occupation of Peking by British and French troops. The setting up of foreign Legations was thereupon finally conceded. The recognition of the equal rights of foreign nations with China which this arrangement expressed was a decisive violation of Chinese fundamental principles (*t'i-chih*) and was probably the greatest loss of prestige which the ruling dynasty had hitherto suffered.

The treaty also provided for the establishment of Chinese Legations in Western capitals. At first, however, the Chinese government could not make the decision to avail itself of this right. The well-intentioned advice of individual foreign representatives, showing how useful such institutions could be for China, was mistrusted. No one believed that a foreigner would give such advice purely in the interests of China, and without its being to his own advantage. The same view is held today by the Chinese Communist government. It was only gradually recognised by a few prudent Chinese statesmen that permanent representatives abroad could be of use because, being in direct contact with a foreign government, they could prevent or at least limit many arbitrary actions and encroachments on the part of foreign representatives in China. But at first no official of sufficient rank could be found who was willing to take on such a difficult task abroad. For the only reward he would receive for this at home would be insults and derision. The greater part of the educated and official class, who formed 'public opinion', inclined to the view that anyone who entered into a close relationship with the barbarians or actually travelled to their country was to be regarded as betraying the 'fundamental principles' of China. Thus the Chinese were content at first to send special temporary delegations which visited the most important Western capitals in turn. Not until 1876 did the Chinese government decide to establish a permanent representative in London, and soon after in other European countries. There were many among the early ambassadors who rapidly grasped the Western view of international relations. They were able in part to represent the interests of China with skill and dignity under difficult conditions, and were accorded considerable respect in the countries where they worked. But the very ones whose reputation was greatest abroad were subjected to the hatred and envy against nonconformists which were displayed by the narrow-minded scholars and officials at home, and some of them ended their days in bitterness and loneliness.

As a result of the unequal treaties, China became, by force and not by her own free choice, a member of the international community of sovereign states which at that time was exclusively controlled by the West. China was no longer the centre of the East Asian family of nations, but became instead a member—at first only of an inferior rank—of a larger family of nations which at that time was exclusively centred on Europe.

3. THE CHRISTIAN MISSIONS IN CHINA

One of the provisions of the 'unequal treaties' was the readmission of the Christian missions and foreign missionaries into China. During the late Ming period and the early Ch'ing period the Catholic mission of the Jesuits under Matteo Ricci and his successors had had considerable success for a time, but was not able to maintain the same level of achievement for long (cf. Ch. IV, §1 above). There was nevertheless a fundamental difference between that early mission and those which followed the Opium War. In the case of the missionaries of the 16th, 17th and 18th centuries, they had always depended upon individual personalities, and there was no political power behind them. Thus the success or failure of their work essentially depended upon the personal skill of the missionaries and their adaptability to Chinese circumstances. After the middle of the 19th century this was no longer so. The missionaries now came to China under the protection of the colonial Powers and were no longer obliged, as Ricci had been, to adapt themselves to Chinese ways in every respect if they wished to remain in the country. Thus their attitude to the Chinese was fundamentally different to that of their predecessors in the 16th and 17th centuries. All the basic difficulties which had stood in the way of the previous missionaries were now encountered to a much greater extent (cf. Ch. IV, §4 above). The Treaty of Nanking contained no provisions concerning the missionaries or their activities. But as early as 1844 and 1846 the French obtained an imperial decree proclaiming the toleration of the Christian religion throughout China. Nevertheless, foreigners were still expressly forbidden to leave the territory of the treaty ports for missionary purposes. With this first official intervention, France began to extend to China her role as the protector of Christian missions, and in particular of Roman Catholic missions. In the years that followed France often exercised her full national authority to protect the Christian religion and the missionaries, and did not hesitate to intervene by force of arms. Other governments also followed the example of France from time to time, and permitted their consuls to force through local demands under the protection of gunboats. In fact, of course, the Western Powers did great harm to Christianity in China by this confusion of national authority and religion. The inevitable consequence was that the Chinese, who were already distrustful by nature of any religious teaching introduced from abroad (cf. Ch. IV, §4 above) now came to regard Christianity as in the first place a tool of the political interests of the Western Powers, and not as a religious faith. For most of the Chinese, opium and Christianity were two evils which had each been introduced in the same way, by trickery and by force, by the foreigners into China. As early as the year 1843 we can see a good example of this pernicious association between the opium trade and the Christian mission. In that year a ship belonging to Jardine, Matheson & Co. sailed into the region north of Amoy with the well-known missionary Dr. Karl Gützlaff on board as interpreter. From one side of the ship, Dr. Gützlaff distributed Christian tracts to the Chinese, while opium was unloaded from the other side.

In spite of the provisions of the imperial decrees of 1844–46, quite a number of foreign missionaries travelled inland. It thus came about in 1856 that in a region of Kuangsi Province that was much disturbed by the Taiping rebellion, a French priest was seized by the local Chinese authorities and killed. This occurrence was one of the excuses for the military intervention on the part of Britain and France which we have already mentioned, and which resulted in the Treaties of Tientsin. The treaties made with Britain, France, America and Russia all contained provisions which expressly permitted the unhindered practice and propagation of the Christian religion throughout China. Particularly grave consequences followed from the provision that not only the foreign missionaries but also the unhindered practice of their religion by native Christians was protected by the treaties, which the foreign Powers were able to ensure were carried out by the presence of their gunboats. This was a significant violation of Chinese sovereignty, and one of its results was that Chinese Christians who were brought to trial for any misdeed could proclaim that they were being persecuted for their Christian religion and turn for help to their own missionaries. The latter often showed themselves all too willing to ask the Legation or consulate of their country to intervene on behalf of the Chinese concerned, on the basis of the treaties of 1858. Apart from this, the missionaries at first found a sympathetic audience and made conversions almost exclusively in circles which were on the edge of or even opposed to the established social order (cf. Ch. IV, §4). Many hoped to gain material advantage from being Christians—the so-called 'rice Christians'. This was often taken so far that Chinese who had been convicted of some punishable offence became Christians as a pure formality in order to place themselves under the protection of the foreigners. This misuse of the Christian doctrine in fact often gave the missionaries a more influential status in the place where their mission was situated than the local *Shen-shih* possessed. But it also had the effect of making it easy for the *Shen-shih*, who were concerned for their own prestige, to influence the mass of people, who would otherwise have been rather indifferent to the whole matter, in their own direction. Hatred and contempt for the Christian religion and its representatives, who under the protection of the treaties were becoming more and more numerous in China, grew stronger, and led to many, frequently violent, outbursts against missionaries and Chinese Christians. In one case a magistrate, harried by the foreign missionaries, concluded that his only defence was to cut his throat in the mission building—according to Chinese customs the severest form of protest—and thus to incite the enraged mob to attack the mission.[1] Almost every outburst against a mission was followed by demands for reparation and an indemnity, often

---

[1] Otto Franke, *Ostasiatische Neubildungen*, Hamburg 1911, p. 172 n. 1.

exacted by force, which increased even more the aversion and hatred for the missionaries.

In the Peking Convention of 1860, after negotiations had been concluded, a clause was slipped into the treaty with France, which conceded the right to the French Catholic missionaries 'to lease and buy land in all provinces, in order to put up buildings there according to their wishes'. This clause led to numerous disputes between the Catholic mission and the official French representatives who made themselves responsible for their interests on the one hand, and the Chinese authorities on the other. Ultimately, the Chinese had to yield to force and recognise the legality of the clause. Thus in Chinese eyes the spread of Christianity in China was tainted not only by its association with the political use of force in the colonising activity of the Great Powers of the West, but also by deceit. In this clause in the French treaty the Protestant missionaries were of course not explicitly included; but on the basis of the 'most favoured nation clause' they were able to establish themselves to an increasing extent inland. The American-Chinese trade treaty of 1903 was the first written document to give Protestant missionaries the right to buy land outside the treaty ports.

These privileges obtained for the foreign missionaries through the 'unequal treaties' were in themselves a very damaging stain on the reputation of the Christian religion in China. The position was made considerably worse by the thoughtless and complacent behaviour of the greater part of the missionaries of all denominations—apart from a small number of honourable exceptions. The understanding and open-minded attitude to China and Chinese civilisation displayed by the West in the 16th and 17th centuries had gradually changed and ultimately deteriorated to the very opposite (cf. Ch. IV, §4 above). Even the missionaries were in the grip of the spirit of their time. With a quite unchristian obtuseness, they tended only too easily to look down upon the Chinese as uncivilised heathen, or even to set them upon the same level as the primitive natives of Africa and the South

Seas. The writings of many missionaries of the 19th and even of the 20th century are distinguished by an incomprehending, tendentious and contemptuous condemnation of the Chinese and their civilisation. Thus for example a German Protestant missionary could write in 1905:

> At a superficial glance—it must be admitted—much in China does not look too bad. It is understandable that Europeans who have been able to keep away from the curiously compounded and very often very penetrating Chinese smells have become admirers of China. . . .
>
> This (i.e. the veneration of ancestors and filial piety) has dazzled and enchanted many of the Europeans who have come to China. But just think. The Chinese no longer realise that love is a commandment of God and in all its manifestations, should be an act of worship, and that piety and obedience towards parents and those set over us are meant to praise and glorify God's moral providence. Since the Chinese no longer realise this, what have they made of the fifth commandment? In a completely heathen way they too have descended to worshipping the creature rather than the creator; at the graves of their ancestors they practise idolatry with the bones of the dead, and offer sacrifices in the memorial halls of their forefathers. . . .
>
> And since the Confucian principle of filial love is identified with the worship of ancestors, from a critical point of view it is nothing more than the biggest humbug that any nation has ever allowed to be imposed upon it. . .[1]

The practical effect of Western missionary policy was that Chinese who were converted to Christianity had to make a substantial break with their traditional customs and usages, that is, with their previous environment. For the 19th century missionaries no longer saw any reason to adapt Christianity to Chinese circumstances even in its external features. A Chinese Christian therefore worshipped a foreign God and became a member of a foreign religious community, in which there was no place for Chinese customs. He became alienated from his own people and his own civilisation. Any kind of concession on the part of foreign missionaries to the peculiar

[1] Otto Reiniger (missionary of the Berliner Missionsgesellschaft in China), *Die Macht des Aberglaubens in China*, Berlin 1905, pp. 4–6.

circumstances of China was unthinkable. Thus Chinese Christians came to be regarded by those around them as already half-foreigners. They did of course come under foreign protection. The Christian missions and their adherents came close to forming a state within the state. The natural consequence of this was constant friction between the missions and the Chinese authorities and local population. A very significant statement is attributed to an important Chinese official, who was himself entirely open-minded; in 1869 he is reported to have said to the English ambassador, 'Take away your opium and your missionaries, and you will be welcome'.[1] The opium trade and the missions were both protected in the same way by the foreigners, and both lay outside the jurisdiction of Chinese law.

In 1870 eighteen French subjects—amongst them ten nuns and the French consul—died in the so-called 'Tientsin Massacre', which arose over a dispute concerning a Catholic orphanage. On account of the stories that had been current about the Portuguese, who were supposed to have eaten little children (cf. Ch. III, §3 above), the mission orphanages were regarded with particular distrust. In their pious zeal the foreign nuns took in children who were already on the point of death, in order to baptise them before they died. Thus a comparatively large proportion of the children who were taken into the orphanages died there. This gave good ground for the rumours and horrifying tales that the foreigners kidnapped or bought little children in order to take their eyes out and make medicine out of them, and so forth. As a result of the 'Tientsin Massacre' the Chinese government sent a memorandum to the representatives of the foreign Powers suggesting that they take precautions against similar occurrences by controlling more strictly the activities of the missions. The government had little influence on uprisings against the missions, which it was very easy for the local *Shen-shih* to incite, for the reasons we have already given (Ch. IV, §4 above). The suggestions made by the Chinese government, however, were incomprehensible

[1] H. B. Morse, *The International Relations of the Chinese Empire* II, pp. 220 f.

to the governments of the Powers concerned. They had little idea of the social structure of China and the ease with which popular feeling could be stirred up. Quite soon, however, voices were raised amongst the missionaries themselves, especially in the Protestant missions, which pointed to the way in which the association of the missions with the colonial and political interests of the Western Powers in China compromised their work, and which called for the removal of the missions from the protection of treaties that had been imposed by force. But these protests remained few and isolated, and had no effect upon the strategy of the mission.

The increasing activity of the Western Powers in the last decade of the 19th century went hand in hand with notable advances on the part of the missions. The Catholic mission in Shantung Province, which consisted predominantly of Germans, withdrew from the traditional protection of France and in 1890 placed itself under the protection of the German Empire, which energetically encouraged the spread of the mission. The murder of two German missionaries in Shantung in the year 1897 gave the German government a most welcome and long-sought-for pretext to occupy the Kiaochou region. The military intervention of the Western Powers on the occasion of the Boxer Rising in 1900, which was largely provoked by the activity of the missionaries, once again demonstrated to the Chinese the identity of the Christian mission and political power. The address given by Kaiser Wilhelm II to the German Expeditionary Force before it embarked for China is characteristic of the spirit of this period:

... So I now send you forth to avenge this wrong, and I shall not rest until the German flags, united with those of the other Powers, float victoriously over those of the Chinese, and planted upon the walls of Peking, impose peace upon the Chinese . . . Russians, Englishmen, Frenchmen, whatever they may be, they are all fighting for one thing, for civilisation. We must think too of something higher, of our religion and the defence and protection of our brothers out there, some of whom have given their lives for their Saviour. . . .

After the overthrow of the Boxer Rising, not only the foreigners, but also many Chinese Christians, encouraged by this visible demonstration of foreign power, sought to obtain restitution from their non-Christian compatriots for the damage inflicted on them in the course of their troubles.

Very slowly, the way was prepared for a change in missionary practice, in the final years before the revolution of 1911. First, the Protestant missions, and then the Catholic missions also, laid the main emphasis in their work on the building and maintenance of hospitals and schools of every sort (kindergarten, primary schools, secondary schools and colleges). Schools which had originally been set up only for Chinese Christians were opened to all Chinese. In this way, the missions also gradually came into contact with members of the educated classes. It was particularly through the mission schools that Western ideas were spread in China. An increasingly Western education and outlook and, in consequence of this, nationalism on the Western pattern became more and more widespread even amongst Chinese Christians. This obliged the missionaries to adopt at least formally a more reserved attitude.

When the political activity of the Western Powers in China ceased to advance and later declined after the first World War, the direct association between politics and the missionaries gradually disappeared. Wholly Chinese Protestant Churches, independent of foreign countries, came into being, and in those which remained dependent on abroad, the Chinese began to play an increasingly decisive part in their leadership—admittedly often in a purely formal sense. In 1946 Rome proclaimed the Catholic Church of China an independent member of the Catholic hierarchy; a Chinese cardinal and several Chinese archbishops were appointed. There had already been Chinese bishops since 1926. In 1950 there were in China approximately $3\frac{1}{4}$ million Catholics and about half a million Protestants, amounting altogether to less than 1 per cent of the whole population of the country.

By the 1940s at the latest Ricci's approach had once again become predominant in both Churches. It was now felt that the native Chinese churches could stand on their own feet and should consequently have a distinctive Chinese form, with the aim that foreign missionaries would finally be able to leave China altogether some day. This realisation came very late, probably too late. There had, it is true, been no lack of warnings during the previous decades. As early as 1906 Otto Franke recognised the situation very clearly when he wrote:

> The missionary question has been handled by official circles in Europe with an indifference which completely belies its real importance. This can only be explained by inadequate knowledge of the basis and character of the Chinese state and society. The greatest, most persistent and most damaging mistake committed by Western diplomacy with regard to China, a mistake of which all the Great Powers have been guilty in spite of all their vigorous assertions to the contrary, was that of using the missionaries as tools in political machinations and as the bearers of political influence. Such a system might have been of value in other parts of the earth, but in China it was clearly pernicious: it became a source of mistrust, hatred and innumerable outrages, and struck a blow against the spread of Christian religion from which it will never recover.[1]

The prophecy contained in the end of this statement was to be confirmed in the events that followed the second World War.

4.   WESTERN DOMINANCE IN CHINA

The Western hegemony guaranteed by the provisions of the 'unequal treaties' gradually reduced China to a semi-colonial status. In practice, not only areas owned or leased by foreign countries but also the concessions and settlements under foreign administration in the treaty ports, and the legation quarters of Peking, were foreign colonies. The number of treaty ports increased from five opened under the 'Treaty of Nanking' to more than thirty-five at the end of the century. The first concessions were granted to Britain in 1859. Towards the end of the century, there were eight British, four French,

[1] Otto Franke, *Ostasiatische Neubildungen*, pp. 174–175.

two Russian and two German concessions, and an Austrian, an Italian and a Belgian concession in nine different treaty ports, to which were added at the turn of the century Japanese concessions, which after the conclusion of the Russo-Japanese war numbered ten. There were also international settlements in seven cities. Many were small and of little significance. But in Shanghai and Tientsin they included the greater part of the city.

In the foreign establishments outside the areas which came under foreign jurisdiction—principally the larger missionary headquarters, since apart from these foreigners were not permitted to possess land outside the concessions and settlements—the colonial atmosphere of the treaty ports also largely prevailed. For here too, because of their right of extra-territoriality, the foreigners were outside the jurisdiction of the Chinese authorities. Any individual foreigner regarded himself anywhere in China as a colonial ruler, and consequently looked down upon the natives as a category of persons essentially far inferior to himself. An enormous difference in the treatment of foreign and native employees was a natural consequence of this underlying attitude. An unimportant foreign employee without any particular qualifications, occupying a subordinate position in a foreign business, could lead a luxurious life by comparison with his circumstances at home or with those of a Chinese holding a similar post. The lower the educational standard of the foreigner, the higher, as a rule, was his presumption and arrogance towards the Chinese. In disputes between foreigners and Chinese the consular courts or similar institutions were the competent authority. In these, the foreigners possessed a fundamental advantage over the Chinese, who were unacquainted with the legal principles that were applied. And quite frequently, a biased judgement was given in any case in favour of the foreigner involved.

The foreigners lived almost entirely on their own, largely separate from their Chinese environment. Thus in a description of the foreign concessions in Canton in the year 1886 we read:

The European colony on Shamin forms a little kingdom in itself. The island is scarcely three thousand feet long, and less than one thousand feet wide, and is separated from the city by a canal; in the years 1859 to 1862, up to which time it had been a marshy island surrounded by mud banks, it was built by the Chinese government at the cost of 325,000 Mexican dollars, and handed over to the British and French governments as settlements. The island is consequently divided into a British settlement, which is larger, and a French settlement which takes up about a fifth of the island. In the British section, members of other nations, such as Germans, Americans and Dutchmen have settled. Leafy avenues, luxurious lawns for playing tennis, beautiful gardens, well-kept pavements and beautifully constructed houses surrounded by wide verandahs adorn the island. Here are the offices and homes of the Europeans, the consulates, an international club and the little church; the whole forms an idyllic corner of the earth, separated from the dirt, the noise, and the foul smell of the nearby Chinese city.[1]

The links between the foreigners and Chinese officials or business men were restricted to the indispensable minimum of contact necessary for commercial and diplomatic business to be carried out. Besides, no Chinese who had some self-respect would have sunk so low as to be involved in social intercourse with the despised and uncivilised foreigners. Thus the contact between the foreigners and their Chinese environment was essentially limited to their domestic servants and to the Chinese employees of their own firms or other businesses. In the foreign firms the foreigners only had direct dealings with one leading Chinese known as the *comprador*. The *comprador* was responsible for the Chinese branch of the firm, and for Chinese business dealings. Quite often the *compradors* contrived to use their prominent position and direct association with the foreigners to their own advantage and amassed considerable fortunes. Consequently, especially later on, they came to be despised as 'slaves of the foreigners' (*yang nu*).

Communication between foreigners and the Chinese was carried out in Pidgin English, a mixture of Portuguese, Chinese

[1] A. H. Exner, *China*, Leipzig 1889, pp. 5–6.

and English. The grammar, and especially the order of words, followed Chinese, while the vocabulary was largely English.

In the treaty ports it was regarded as practically impossible to learn Chinese. According to the views current at that time, which prevailed far into the 20th century, to learn Chinese demanded 'a head of oak, lungs of brass, nerves of steel, a constitution of iron, the patience of Job, and the lifetime of Methuselah'.[1]

In the treaty ports the foreigners developed a distinctive colonial style of life with little work, and much, frequently monotonous, entertainment, which consisted above all of very sumptuous revelling and banqueting. The stimulus and variety which their Chinese environment could have offered was virtually inaccessible to them. As a rule, they were not interested in it. Most of them lacked sufficient understanding to enjoy the Chinese theatre, Chinese food and other refinements of Chinese civilisation. Here, for example, is a description of the life of a foreigner in Tientsin in the year 1886:

> . . . Apart from this business activity, which only requires our attention now and again, we spend our time in the way of life which is usual here, which must be described as on the whole exceedingly monotonous. . . . The comparatively few Europeans who live here have no one else to turn to but themselves in their social intercourse . . . and thus as a rule each day goes by like all the others. In the early morning an hour or two is spent at work, and in the afternoon, when the heat permits, one can play lawn tennis with the few ladies in the colony, and it is possible to take a ride later on into the monotonous area of the town nearby or perhaps beyond the mud wall of the city to the settlement race-course, which lies in the open country and is completely without shade. Towards mid-day one meets the other men in the club for whisky and soda, and to hear the gossip of the town, and in the evening there will be a game of billiards or skittles in the same place. . . . Since the "real" work is usually restricted for Europeans, as in most places overseas, to a few days in the week, that is, to the days round about the arrival and departure of the mail steamer, they have an extraordinary amount of free time left at

[1] C. F. Gordon Cumming, *Wanderings in China*, Edinburgh and London 1886, II, 54. Quoted from J. K. Fairbank, *Trade and Diplomacy on the China Coast*, Cambridge, Mass., 1953, p. 14 n. b.

their disposal, which in the absence of any opportunity for intellectual amusement, tends largely to be spent in entertaining and being entertained at extraordinarily opulent dinners and suppers.[1]

By far the greatest international colony was that of the great international settlement and the somewhat smaller French concession in Shanghai. In a city which before it was opened as a treaty port was of little significance, the foreign population rapidly grew from 150 in 1850 to almost 4,000 in 1890, and over 10,000 in 1910. Thus there was a great deal more variety amongst the foreigners in Shanghai, and in their interests, than in the other treaty ports, so that the monotony described in the passage quoted above did not apply to Shanghai. Shanghai formed the pattern for other ports. The spirit of initiative and enterprise also spread to the rapidly increasingly Chinese population of Shanghai. Even today, when there are scarcely any foreigners living there and all private businesses have been nationalised, the inhabitants of Shanghai are amongst the most active and enterprising in the whole of China.

The legation quarter of Peking represented a different kind of foreign settlement. Here the tone was set by the diplomats; business men played no part at first, and a very subordinate part later on. Furthermore, in Peking contact with the Chinese environment, while it was certainly not very intensive, was not altogether so minimal as in the concessions and settlements in the ports.

The front presented by the foreigners to the Chinese, however, was not so unified as it might seem at first glance, and as it has always been represented. In the case of the British in particular, who in fact, as we have said, had the widest interests in China and formed the majority of the foreigners, a permanent conflict existed from the time of the Opium War right into the 20th century between the merchants, the so-called 'old China hands'—on whose side were also a large proportion of the missionaries—and the representatives of the Foreign Office. Sometimes this conflict became acute. The British

[1] A. H. Exner, *China*, p. 27.

merchants and the foreign colonies as a whole at the treaty
orts held firmly to the idea that in view of the size of China's
population, the Chinese market provided almost unlimited
possibilities for the spread of foreign trade, if only the necessary
political conditions and requirements were satisfied. They
wanted, as it were, to convert the whole of China into an
enormous treaty port under foreign control. Consequently,
they demanded from the government at home and its representatives in China an energetic approach to the Chinese, and a
constant readiness to take military action, in order to extend
the influence of British trading interests. The intention was to
make the whole of China, or at least the Yangtse provinces,
into a second India.

By contrast with this somewhat emotional wishful thinking
the better educated and more far-sighted diplomatic representatives usually adopted realistic attitudes. They were more
or less firmly supported in this by the government departments
concerned and by public opinion at home. Of course they were
also concerned to extend British trade and to advance British
interests. But they held a very much less favourable view of
the prospects of British trade with China than the 'old China
hands'. This judgement was not made on political grounds,
but with regard to economic conditions in China, which made
possible a high degree of internal self-sufficiency and left very
little scope for trade from outside. The British diplomats saw
quite clearly that if China was to become a second India, it
would create immense difficulties for Britain and demand
enormous expenditure, which would bear no relation to what
they could hope to gain. The progressive tendency towards
collapse manifested by the Chinese central government after
the Taiping rebellion caused great anxiety to the British
government, which feared nothing more than this. Such a
collapse would probably have made it necessary for England
to take over the administration of the whole of China, or of
large areas of the country, if it was not to fall into the hands of
other European Powers. Thus the fundamental aim of British
policy in China was the preservation of the Chinese central

G

government and the strengthening of its authority. The desires and requests of foreigners should not be carried out—as the merchants wished, and as often happened in fact—by the use of force against the local Chinese authorities, but instead, the central government in Peking should be made responsible for carrying out all measures laid down in the treaties throughout the whole Empire. Many of the British representatives had a sensitive understanding of the Chinese situation. Sometimes they even accorded more sympathy and respect to Chinese civilisation than their compatriots in the treaty ports, as did Sir Rutherford Alcock, the minister from 1866 on, during the T'ungchih Restoration, or his successor Sir Thomas Wade, later the first professor of Sinology at the University of Cambridge. The American envoy Burlingame, later entrusted by the Chinese government with an official mission to Europe and America, and the first Inspector-General of the Imperial Maritime Customs, Sir Robert Hart, who held the post for a very long period, belonged to this group. They all stood to a certain extent between the 'old China hands' and the Chinese government. In the gossip of the treaty ports Wade, Hart, Burlingame and Wells Williams, for a time the American chargé d'affaires and the author of what used to be the standard work on China, *The Middle Kingdom*, came to be known as the 'tough "Quadrilateral" which defends more effectually than have done the Taku Forts, Chinese arrogance, pride, and exclusiveness against the inroads of Western civilisation'.[1] Here again we can see the extraordinary degree to which relations between China and the West depended on individual personalities (cf. Ch. IV, §4 above). All too often, however, personalities such as these, who were able to achieve a certain sympathy with the Chinese, and were therefore able to make some progress, were regarded with suspicion and mistrust by their own compatriots or by the departments at home under which they served. It is true, of course, that such factors are generally at work in relationships between different nations. But in dealings with the Chinese, as with those who belong to

[1] Gumpach, *The Burlingame Mission*, Shanghai 1872, pp. 236–237.

other East Asian nations, the importance of personal adaptability cannot be over-estimated.

The organisation of the Imperial Maritime Customs by official British representatives was violently opposed by the 'old China hands'. It is true that this Maritime Customs Department, under the direction and control of foreigners, bore the marks of foreign domination. But it must in fact be regarded as a special joint institution common to the Chinese and the foreigners. The Inspector-General and the whole foreign section of the service were Chinese officials with an appropriate Chinese rank, and as such were directly subordinate to the Chinese Emperor. By creating and keeping in being an institution which carried out its work in an incorrupt and trustworthy way, Sir Robert Hart and his successors carried out their duty towards the Chinese government as they understood it. They defended the interests of the Chinese government and enforced the payment by foreign traders—who frequently resisted—of the customs duties established by the treaties. Only an institution controlled by foreigners possessed the authority to do this. A purely Chinese customs organisation would at that time have been largely powerless against the arrogance of the foreigners, and in addition would immediately have been corrupted. Thus the money conveyed to the Chinese government from maritime customs duties became an increasingly important and reliable source of income for the Chinese government. A few far-seeing persons on the Chinese side in fact recognised the importance of the Imperial Maritime Customs, and of foreign advisers in other posts, and did their best to co-operate with them. As a result, these Chinese officials were widely attacked by less perspicacious and more conservative officials and scholars, as violently, or sometimes even more violently, than were the foreigners who co-operated with the Chinese, by the 'old China hands' at the treaty ports. Like the British Civil Service in India, the Imperial Maritime Customs and other institutions under foreign control in China developed a distinctive attitude of their own, which does not fit into the over-simplified categories of a theory of imperialism that sees everything as either black or white.

VI

China's Response to the Challenge of the West

1. THE PREVAILING IDEAS OF THE WEST IN CHINA AND THE
CHINESE ATTITUDE TO THE WEST UP TO THE END OF THE
T'UNGCHIH RESTORATION

During the late Ming period and the early Ch'ing period a
number of particularly open-minded persons amongst the
leading intellectual circles of China—including the first two
Manchu Emperors themselves—showed great interest in the
West and in its intellectual life. Amongst others, Matteo
Ricci made an important contribution to their knowledge of
world geography by his map of the world, with place names
written in Chinese, which he published in 1602. On this map
the different European countries were drawn with considerable
accuracy, so that one could obtain from this map a fairly clear
idea of their position. As in the West, interest in the world
abroad and in its civilisation disappeared in China after the end
of the 17th century, and even the knowledge conveyed by
Ricci was largely forgotten. As late as the beginning of the
Opium War, for example, there was still considerable confusion
about the different European countries and their relationship
to one another. Thus the Portuguese, known as 'Folangchi'
(cf. n. 1, p. 21), were confused with the French, known as
'Falanhsi'. Since many of the Jesuit missionaries who came to
China through the Portuguese settlement at Macao were
Italian, and since in particular their superiors lived in Italy,
'Italiya' was also regarded as the home country of the Portuguese in Macao. This produced further confusion when in the
1840s real Italians from 'Itali' appeared in China. Just as for
the average European, Chinese, Japanese, and Koreans can
scarcely be distinguished from each other, so the different
Europeans were basically the same to the Chinese. Thus, for

example, the Dutch and the English were both known as 'red-haired barbarians' (*hung-mao fan*) without distinction.

It is known that in the 17th and 18th centuries a number of Chinese came to Europe, and some of them returned to China. But with one not very fruitful exception, none of them have left accounts of their experiences in the West. One reason for this was probably the fundamental prohibition, applying to all Chinese, against leaving China. And in general the view of China's relationship to foreign peoples which we have already described, and the traditional contempt for barbarians, prevented anyone giving a thorough and conscientious account of them. The Europeans were regarded as barbarians in the same way as the peoples of Central Asia or South-East Asia, and the Dutch and British embassies were entered in official chronicles and handbooks as 'tribute embassies' in the same way as those of the Asian countries. Thus the few descriptions that existed of Europe and its inhabitants were still a mixture of truth and legend even in the middle of the 19th century. They often gave excessive weight to trivial outward peculiarities, which had seemed noteworthy to the Chinese observer. The same phenomenon occurs, of course, in Western descriptions of the Chinese. In this connection, an illustrated work from the middle of the 18th century on the Chinese tribute nations (*Huang Ch'ing chih-kung t'u*) is of particular interest, for it contains drawings and descriptions of a number of European countries. The illustrations in it have apparently been prepared from European originals. Germany is not mentioned in it, nor is Holland, which was known to the Chinese by their direct contact with the Dutch; but there is a passage on Switzerland which reads:

The province of Helvetia (*Ho-lo-wei-chi-ya*) lies in the country Germany (*Jo-erh-ma-ni-ya*). Its inhabitants are strong and broad in stature. They are loyal and honest. When they benefit from a good action, they repay it. In each community public schools have been established. Well over half [of the Swiss] undergo military training. They like to travel to other countries, whose princes used them as guards. The country is very mountainous and very cold in the winter months. [The Swiss] are very good at building houses. Their women are virtuous, quiet, and straightforward in their demeanour. They are skilful workers and are able to weave gilded cloth using their hands alone, and without using a shuttle. Their fabrics are extremely light and fine. The ground produces gold. They dig shafts and constantly obtain nuggets of gold from them. In the river-beds there are frequently pearls of gold as large as a pea. In the mountains there are stags, deer, hare and wild cats. They breed great cattle, which they use for a delicacy.[1]

The following description is given of England:

England is a country which belongs to Holland. The clothing and appearance of the barbarians is much the same in every part of the country. The country is quite rich. The men mostly wear woollen cloth, and like to drink wine. The unmarried women lace up their hips in their desire to be slim. They wear their hair falling loosely over the shoulder, with short clothes and several coats one above the other. When they go out they put on an overcoat over them all. They keep snuff in metallic wire boxes and carry them about with them.[2]

The only known Chinese writing which was published before the Opium War on the basis of direct experience was 'A Maritime Record' (Hai-lu). It is the account, written down by a scholar, of a Chinese sailor who in the last two decades of the 18th century travelled on foreign ships, probably Portuguese for the most part, to the principal trading ports of the world, including those of Europe and America. The descriptions are in fact very brief and almost without exception give dry factual information, but hardly any personal impressions or judgements. Only the accounts of Portugal and England are somewhat longer, and basically correct in their detail. Germany is not mentioned, but the description of Holland is as follows:

Holland is the region in the north-west of France. The people and their clothing are all the same as in Portugal. Rich people

---

[1] *Huang Ch'ing chih-kung t'u* 1, 35a.
[2] ibid. 1, 47a.

extensive pasture lands. There are 57,000 horses, 275,000 cattle and 345,000 sheep. Through this country the great river Danube flows. The capital is called Vienna; it has 300,000 inhabitants, who are very skilled in the manufacture of cotton and silken cloth. The king's palace is particularly magnificent; [the king] however, is personally frugal. He deals with his people as a father with his children, and treats others in a friendly way. The people cling steadfastly to the Catholic religion. They particularly hate the doctrine of evil spirits and of geomancy [*feng-shui*]. [The people] love to drink, and to listen to music. The women are cheerful and pretty, but do not maintain their chastity. The suburb [of Vienna] has 36,000 inhabitants. In the library there are 70,000 volumes. In a nearby city there is a shrine, where the people burn incense and venerate images. Deluded by the priests, they have made gold and silver furnishings [for the shrines].—One [part of the country] is called Tyrol. It lies in the mountains. Its inhabitants are upright, and are fond of hunting. When the French invaded this country, the population fought back the enemy in battle. Because the mountain country is stony and infertile [the inhabitants] often leave it for other regions.—One [part of the country] is called Illyria, the southern part of which extends to the Adriatic Sea. It contains many mountains, caves and valleys. The capital is called Laibach; it has over 40,000 inhabitants. They make porcelain and manufacture satin. The port [of this province] is called Trieste; it is visited by 8,000 ships every year . . .' (This is followed by a description of other parts of the country.)

Bavaria: This is a region in the South. In the East it borders on Austria. Its area is 90,000 square *li* and it has four million inhabitants. They have a high regard for old customs, and are obstinate and stubborn. The Prince of this province has recently set up an academy to take scholarly and wise men, in order to advance education. . . .

Then the capital, Munich, and other towns, Nürnberg, Landshut, Regensburg and Augsburg are briefly described. The names of provinces and towns are sometimes transcribed into Chinese according to their sound, and sometimes according to their meaning: Nilin Shan, 'Nilin Mountain'=Nürnberg, and Yü-shan, 'Rain Mountain'=Regensburg. Then Württemberg and Baden and their capitals are described, and then comes:

Saxony: In the south it borders on Bavaria and Austria. The northern part produces different sorts of gold, silver and tin. Although the silver mines have already been worked for 500 years, they are not yet exhausted. In olden times all Germany's jewellery came from these mountains. The population of these mountains is short of corn; [consequently] they live by mining in the summer, while in the winter they travel about performing music. The customs of the people in the North are joyful; they are upright and not deceitful. They can make woollen fabric out of the finest sheep's wool. In addition, they manufacture porcelain goods, which are better than those of the Chinese. The capital is called Dresden. The Royal Palace and the Catholic Church, as well as the houses which collect antiquities [i.e. the museums] are more beautiful than in other countries. In Leipzig there is a fair twice a year and all merchants congregate there. In particular, there are numerous books from all regions. There are tens of thousands of old books and new books there, too many to count. The wares exchanged there are worth 3 million *tael*. . . .

Then the Thuringian states are described in a few sentences, mentioning one or two characteristic features. This is followed by Anhalt, Mecklenburg, Brunswick, Hohenzollern, Liechtenstein, and other small principalities, and then Hanover is treated in somewhat greater detail, including a mention of the university city of Göttingen ('In K'o-t'ing-yen there is a great literary academy from which scholars in academic studies go forth'), Hessen-Kassel, Hessen-Darmstadt, Nassau and Oldenburg. The description concludes:

In Germany there are also other independent cities, which are not subject to any prince. They trade independently and appoint officials to carry out their administration. One of these is called *Hamburg*; it lies at the mouth of the River Elbe. It is a market for all the provinces and merchants congregate there in large numbers. Ships [from Hamburg] also come as far as China to trade. In the year Taokuang 22 (1842) the greater part of the city was burnt down. [Hamburg] has 120,000 inhabitants. The value of the goods which are imported and exports there come to more than 4, 290 ounces of silver.—Another [free city] is called *Bremen*, with 42,000 inhabitants. It lies on the banks of the River Weser. Its ships have also come to Canton to trade.—Another is called

Lübeck; it has 24,000 inhabitants. Although it is an old city, its trade is quite small.—Another is called *Frankfurt*. This is the oldest city. It lies on the banks of a river and is the place where the envoys of all the princes meet together. In [Frankfurt] the defence forces of the [German] states are based. Every year there is a great fair, to which people swarm from every direction.

The longest river in the country is the Rhine. It flows from south to north. In the West of Germany it flows into Holland and there runs into the sea. [It is to the Germans] what the Yellow River is to the Chinese. The fertile banks of the river are famous for the grapes which grow there. Along the river there are many ancient buildings and curiously shaped peaks. Travellers paint pictures of them.—There is also the river Danube, which flows across the country like a belt.—In the North there is the Elbe, as well as other rivers.

The customs of the people of the country vary a great deal because they are subject to different princes. The people in the North are strong-willed and very ready to learn. Those in the South and East are very fond of sumptuous eating and drinking. In the South-West the life of the people is very hard. In their dealings with one another the [German] people are not peaceful; there are constant disputes.[1]

Much more reliable information about the West is given in the geography of the world *Ying-huan chih-lüeh* by Hsü Chi-yü (1795–1873). Hsü had much to do with the foreigners when he was Governor of Fukien in 1847–51, and took advantage of every opportunity that was offered to gather information from them and to procure literature. Hsü's geography of the world is the first Chinese work which drew directly on contemporary Western atlases and took from them the geographical names which were then in use, instead of traditional Chinese terms, many of which had long ceased to be applicable. It also contained full descriptions of the countries of the West, based on contemporary literature. At the same time, all these sources were obtained at second-hand. The author could not make use of his own observations. Thus many things in the West remained incomprehensible to him. By contrast, Western descriptions of China from that period drew on the direct personal experience and observation of the author—as for

[1] *Hai-kuo t'u-chih*, ed. 1880, 44, 17b–22b.

example Wells Williams, *The Middle Kingdom*—and consequently displayed a better understanding in many respects.

The way in which the Chinese were bound by traditional
conceptions made it impossible at that period for them to go
beyond the recording of facts to give a more profound analysis
of the forces that underlay the aggressive advance of the West
and of the true reasons for Western superiority. Thus the
English interpreter Thomas Taylor Meadows, writing in 1852,
described the attitude of the Chinese to foreigners in the following words:

> The Chinese do habitually call and consider Europeans
> "barbarians"; meaning by that term "people in a rude, uncivilized
> state, morally and intellectually uncultivated" . . . Those Chinese
> who have direct opportunities of learning something of our
> customs and culture—they may amount, taking all Five Ports,
> to some five or six thousand out of three hundred and sixty
> millions—mostly consider us beneath their nation in moral and
> intellectual cultivation. As to those who have had no such
> opportunities, I do not recollect conversing with one, and I have
> conversed with many, whose previous notions of us were not
> analogous to those we entertain of savages. They are always
> surprised, not to say astonished, to learn that we have surnames,
> and understand the family distinctions of father, brother, wife,
> sister, etc.; in short, that we live otherwise than as a herd of
> cattle.[1]

The missionary societies were the first to begin to publish
Chinese translations from Western languages—including non-
religious matters. But the educated classes in China despised
the Christian religion and everything that had to do with it.
Thus in these circles the Western literature that was available
was largely ignored up to the end of the century. Furthermore,
the missionaries as a rule only had people of poor education to
help them in their work. Consequently, the style of the translations these people produced left much to be desired. This
was a further reason why the educated class ignored them.
Only when a special department was set up in 1861 to deal
with foreign affairs, the *Tsungli-Yamen*—which corresponded to

[1] Quoted from J. K. Fairbank, *Trade and Diplomacy on the China Coast*, p. 19.

a Ministry of Foreign Affairs—did Chinese government circles begin to feel the necessity for more accurate knowledge of the West. In the same year the establishment of a school for the study of languages, the *T'ung-wen kuan*, was ordered. With the assistance of foreign teaching personnel, it was intended that the government staff be trained in foreign languages there. Different translation institutes were brought into being, and the government commissioned translations of Western books. Apart from works on military matters, ship-building, etc., special interest was shown in Western international law. In the *Tsungli-Yamen* the importance of international law was recognised, and an attempt was made to turn the knowledge gained from translations to the practical advantage of China in her dealings with foreigners. This was successful, for example, in the case of the capture, contrary to international law, of Danish merchant vessels in Chinese territorial waters by the warship of the first Prussian Ambassador von Rehfues in 1864, during the war betwen Prussia and Denmark. In spite of the way in which Western international law was occasionally used to China's advantage in this way, those in authority in the Chinese government were not ready to abandon their traditional ways of thought and their own 'fundamental principles', and allow China to become a member of the Western family of nations as one state with the same rights as all the others. The open mind displayed in the 1860s by a number of leading figures in the T'ungchih restoration by no means signifies that they intended to alter China's traditional system of relations with foreign nations. All reforms had to remain within the traditional framework, and were intended to maintain and strengthen the traditional system. Their intention was in some way to fit the new circumstances created by the treaties and the presence of permanent foreign representatives in Peking, into the traditional order.

'Self-strengthening' (*tzu ch'iang*) was the watchword from the 1860s on, and the slogan 'Chinese learning for the base, Western learning for practical application' (*chung-hsüeh wei t'i, hsi-hsüeh wei yung*) was the guide. As an example, here is an excerpt from a work by Feng Kuei-fen (1809–1874) written in the 1850s. Feng did not himself hold high office, but he was the learned adviser of persons in authority, so that his ideas had considerable influence upon them:

The most unparalleled anger which has ever existed since the creation of heaven and earth is exciting all who are conscious in their minds and have spirit in their blood; their hats are raised by their hair standing on end. This is because the largest country on the globe today, with a vast area of 10,000 *li*, is yet controlled by small nations of barbarians. . . . According to a general geography by an Englishman, the territory of our China is eight times larger than that of Russia, ten times that of America, one hundred times that of France, and two hundred times that of England. . . . Yet now we are shamefully humiliated by those four nations in the recent treaties—not because our climate, soil, or resources are inferior to theirs, but because our people are really inferior. . . . Why are they small and yet strong? Why are we large and yet weak? We must try to discover some means to become their equal, and that also depends upon human effort. Regarding the present situation there are several major points: in making use of the ability of our manpower, with no one neglected, we are inferior to the barbarians; in securing the benefit of the soil, with nothing wasted, we are inferior to the barbarians; in maintaining a close relationship between the ruler and the people, with no barrier between them, we are inferior to the barbarians; and in the necessary accord of word with deed, we are also inferior to the barbarians. The way to correct these four points lies with our-selves, for they can be changed at once if only our Emperor would set the general policy right. There is no need for outside help in these matters. (Here Feng goes on to pointo ut that the only help China needs from the West is in modern arms, and he claims that in recent contests with Western troops the Chinese army has not been inferior in physical qualities, nor even some-times in morale, but always in arms.) What we then have to learn from the barbarians is only the one thing, solid ships and effective guns. When Wei Yüan (in his *Hai-kuo t'u-chih* [see pp. 96-7]) discussed the control of the barbarians, he said that we should use barbarians to attack barbarians, and use barbarians to negotiate with barbarians. Even regardless of the difficulties of language and our ignorance of diplomatic usage it is utterly impossible for us outsiders to sow dissension among the closely related bar-barians. Moreover, he considered the various barbarian nations as comparable to the Warring States (403–221 B.C.), but he did not realize that the circumstances are different. Wei saw quite a number of barbarian books and newspapers and should not have made any such statement. It is probably because in his life and academic ideas he was fond of regarding himself as a political strategist. In my opinion, if we cannot make ourselves strong (tzu-ch'ing) but merely presume on cunning and deceit, it will be just enough to incur failure. Only one sentence of Wei Yuan is correct: "Learn the strong techniques of the barbarians in order to control them".[1]

In the 1860s the whole educated class in China still agreed that the traditional order should be preserved at all costs. But opinions differed greatly as to the best way to do this. Those whose slogan was 'self-strengthening', and who advocated the removal of China's weakness by learning from the barbarians, were violently opposed by the vast majority of scholars and officials. At that period there was no press in China, but there was nevertheless a powerful 'public opinion'. It was formed by the majority of the *Shen-shih* class, both those who were officials and those who were not. These tended to regard anyone who entered into a closer association with the barbarians, or actually visited their country, as a traitor to the 'fundamental principles' of China. The part played by the censors was particularly important. Their task was to superintend the way the officials fulfilled their duties, and they could immediately denounce any attitude that was not in conformity with this 'public opinion'. In Chinese 'public opinion' is known as *ch'ing-i*, 'pure discussion', or more accurately, 'gossipy criticism' from a position of no responsibility. Nevertheless, this public criticism was so powerful that even the Emperor and the highest officials could not avoid it. It was a decisive hindrance to all movements for innovation or reform—even if these were entirely within the framework of the traditional order. For the representatives of this 'public opinion' were irrevocably committed to a traditional intellectual position. They were convinced that every change meant a possible

---

[1] 'Chih yang-ch'i i' in *Chiao-pin-lu k'ang-i* 2, 40–44. Quoted from Teng-Fairbank, *China's Response to the West*, Cambridge, Mass. 1954, pp. 52–53.

infringement on their own position and their own interests. Thus a representative of this point of view (Wo-jen, who died in 1871) wrote as follows in a memorandum to the Emperor against the study of Western knowledge in 1867:

Your slave has learned that the way to establish a nation is to lay emphasis on propriety and righteousness, not on power and plotting. The fundamental effort lies in the minds of people, not in techniques. Now, if we seek trifling arts and respect barbarians as teachers regardless of the possibility that the cunning barbarians may not teach us their essential techniques—even if the teachers sincerely teach and the students faithfully study them, all that can be accomplished is the training of mathematicians. From ancient down to modern times, your slave has never heard of anyone who could use mathematics to raise the nation from a state of decline or to strengthen it in time of weakness. The empire is so great that one should not worry lest there be any lack of abilities therein. If astronomy and mathematics have to be taught, an extensive search should find someone who has mastered the technique. Why is it limited to barbarians and why is it necessary to learn from the barbarians?

Moreover, the barbarians are our enemies. In 1860 they took up arms and rebelled against us. Our capital and its surburb were invaded, our ancestral altar was shaken, our Imperial palace was burned, and our officials and people were killed or wounded. There had never been such insults during the last 200 years of our dynasty. All our scholars and officials have been stirred with heart-burning rage, and have retained their hatred until the present. Our court could not help making peace with the barbarians. How can we forget this enmity and this humiliation even for one single day?

Since the conclusion of the peace, Christianity has been prevalent and half of our ignorant people have been fooled by it. The only thing we can rely on is that our scholars should clearly explain to the people the Confucian tenets, which may be able to sustain the minds of the ignorant populace. Now if these brilliant and talented scholars, who have been trained by the nation and reserved for great future usefulness, have to change from their regular course of study to follow the barbarians, then the correct spirit will not be developed, and accordingly the evil spirit will become stronger. After several years it will end in nothing less than driving the multitudes of the Chinese people into allegiance to the barbarians.

Reverently your slave has read the instruction to the grand councillors and officers of the nine government bureaus in the Collected Essays of the K'ang-hsi Emperor, in which he says, "After a thousand or several hundred years, China must be harmed by the various countries of Europe". The deep and far-reaching concern of the sage Emperor is admirable. Even though he used their methods, he actually hated them. Now, the empire has already been harmed by them. Should we further spread their influence and fan the flame? Your slave has heard that when the barbarians spread their religion, they hate Chinese scholars who are not willing to learn it. Now scholars from the regular channels are ordered to study under foreigners. Your slave fears that what our scholars are going to learn cannot be learnt well and yet will be perplexing, which would just fall in with [the foreigners'] plans. It is earnestly hoped that, in order to maintain the general prestige of the empire and to prevent the development of disaster, the Imperial mind will independently decide to abolish instantly the previous decision to establish such studies in the language school. The whole empire will be fortunate, indeed.[1]

In this case, it is true, Wo-jen's suggestions were not followed. But he remained one of the most influential representatives of the ultra-reactionary movement at court, though we do not know whether he was in good faith, or whether he hoped to gain by this.

In spite of the violent opposition of Wo-jen and his numerous adherents, the more open-minded of those in authority succeeded during the restoration period of the 1860s in temporarily stabilising the relations between China and the West on the basis of the treaties that had been concluded. Their efforts were made easier by the attitude of the foreign ministers in Peking at that time, who looked on the affairs of China with understanding and good will. Ultimately, however, all these efforts failed to bridge the gap between two fundamentally opposed worlds. The demands of a situation completely new to China could no longer be permanently satisfied by the use of traditional means.

---

[1] *Ch'ou-pan i-wu shih-mo*, T'ung-chih, 47, 24–25. Quoted from **Teng-Fairbank,** *China's Response to the West*, pp. 76–77.

H

2. THE BEGINNING OF A FUNDAMENTAL CHANGE IN THE VIEW OF THE WEST AND ITS CIVILISATION: THE REFORM MOVEMENT

Even after the failure of the T'ungchih restoration, the prevailing response to increasing foreign pressure in the 1870s and 1880s was provided by the traditional forms of Chinese resistance and Chinese reaction. According to the traditional view of the relationship of China to foreign nations, China could not make the sharp distinction usual in the West between internal and foreign policy. Rather, relations with the barbarians were a secondary function of the administration of China. 'Disturbance within and attack from outside' (*nei luan wai huan*) followed each other as symptoms of a bad and ineffective government. Thus at that period the underlying reasons for the oppressed situation of China was not seen in Western colonialism and imperialism, but in China's own weakness. And this weakness in its turn was attributed to the lack of able persons, conscious of their responsibilities, in the government of China. According to Chinese traditions the quality of those who conducted the government was the decisive factor in the political situation. A purely secondary significance was attributed to institutions and laws. This one-sided judgement played an essential part in preventing an unprejudiced recognition of the reasons for China's weakness.

The attempt to adopt no more than the technical and military devices on which Western power was built, was bound to fail, because the basic requirements of technological thought, and a social and political structure which could make technical development possible, were lacking. Similarly, the effort to practise an active foreign policy by attempting to play individual Western countries off against each other could offer little hope of success. As a result of the ever more obvious hopelessness of China's weakness against the West, and even against Japan, the morale of the Chinese officials rapidly declined, and this brought about the failure of the movement of 'self-strengthening', the main purpose of which had been to strengthen the moral powers of the Chinese themselves.

In this situation, which constantly grew more desperate for China, a group of young scholars arrived at the conviction that in order to save China from the aggression of the West and Japan, far more extensive measures were necessary than a restoration and the strengthening of the people's moral powers within the traditional framework. This new course is known as the Reform Movement. Its principal exponents were K'ang Yu-wei, T'an Szu-t'ung and Liang Ch'i-ch'ao. They became convinced that it was not enough for China to adopt merely the practical and technical achievements of the West. They regarded as absolutely necessary a change in institutions (*kai chih*) and a law reform (*pien fa*) on the Western pattern. Thus they emphatically opposed the view that had traditionally prevailed, that what mattered in the first place was the men who conducted the government and their personal policy. It is true that the leaders of the Reform Movement were still too much in the grip of the traditional Confucian view of the world and the state for their thought to make a complete break with Confucian traditions—perhaps with the exception of T'an Szu-t'ung, whose ideas were in many respects much more radical than those of the others.

As a scholar brought up on Confucian thought, K'ang Yu-wei, and his supporters with him, turned to the sacred Canonical Writings of Confucianism, to seek in them a way of salvation out of the misfortunes of the present time, and a justification for their plans for reform. Nevertheless, some of the conclusions which K'ang Yu-wei came to in the course of his study of the Canonical Writings were altogether revolutionary for this period. He established that in the course of the last two thousand years the original Confucian tradition had been corrupted and falsified. It was now necessary to go back to the true original of the earliest period and correct the corrupt tradition. K'ang Yu-wei and his friends discovered completely new wisdom in the text of the Canonical Writings, and their view of them came into direct contradiction with the orthodox interpretation of the tradition which had been officially accepted for centuries. They regarded Confucius himself as a religious founder and reformer, and sought by building on this conception to justify their own plans for reform, influenced as they were by the West. In addition, they believed they had discovered references to many institutions and achievements of the West in the Canonical Writings. Furthermore, they drew on numerous non-Confucian philosophers of the pre-Christian period to prove and corroborate their theses. It cannot be known for certain whether they were ever convinced themselves of the soundness of their arguments in individual details, or merely intended to give more weight to their new ideas by appealing to Chinese antiquity. There is no doubt, however, that they were convinced of the fundamental accord between their ideas and the original teaching of Confucius. In accordance with Chinese ways of thought, an occasional obvious discrepancy between the theory and the practical reality did not disconcert them.

Translations of Western texts by foreign missionaries, and also by Chinese institutions, as well as the return of the first Chinese to go abroad to study, and the establishment of permanent Chinese diplomatic representations abroad, led to considerable progress in China's knowledge of the West and its civilisation during the last two decades of the 19th century. Even though K'ang Yu-wei had not yet travelled outside China himself during this period, nevertheless many of his friends already had personal experience of the West, and were able to read Western books and writings in the original. Thus those who belonged to the Reform Movement possessed a far more fundamental and profound understanding of what the West was really like than the best 'experts' twenty years earlier. Consequently, they saw the situation and importance of China with regard to other nations in a completely new light. Statements such as the following already amount to the virtual abandonment of a universalism centred upon China:

The earth does not consist of only one country, and a country does not consist of only one man. Every man has his own mind, and every mind its own knowledge. If one does not examine the general circumstances of different countries, one does not get to know their strong and weak sides. If one does not examine the theories and arguments put forward by different countries, one does not get to know what is good and bad in their intentions. If one does not study the scientific knowledge of different countries, one does not get to know the abilities in which they are skilled or unskilled.[1]

Or:

In the whole earth, China is only one of fifty-six countries. The earth is only one of two hundred and forty-nine planets in the solar system. The sun is only one of the myriads, millions, and milliards of fixed stars, gathered together in heaven like the innumerable grains of sand of the river Ganges, in heaps, clouds, and mists of stars. And in infinite space, heaven is only one of the innumerable, unimaginable grains of sand of the river Ganges.[2]

Or:

A combination of men makes a country. A combination of countries makes the world (*T'ien-hsia*).[3]

Or again, K'ang Yu-wei writes in a somewhat different context:

Today [the states of the world] compete with each other rather like [the separate Chinese states] at the period of the *Spring and Autumn Annals* and the Warring States, and there is no longer a unified rule as under the Han, T'ang, Sung and Ming dynasties. This can only be described as a change unknown for thousands of years.[4]

Here, then, K'ang Yu-wei sees the different nations of the

[1] By Shou-fu. Quoted from W. Franke, 'Die staatspolitischen Reformversuche K'ang Yu-weis und seiner Schule', *Mitteilungen des Seminars für Orientalische Sprachen Berlin, Ostasiatische Studien* 38, 1935, p. 24.

[2] By Mai Meng-hua. Quoted from W. Franke, op. cit. p. 24.

[3] By Liu Chen-lin, 'Ti-ch'iu liu ta tsui-an k'ao tsung-hsü', *Huang-ch'ao ching-shih wen hsin-pien*, ed. 1898, ch. 18b, 17b.

[4] *Wu hsü pien-fa (Chung-kuo chin-tai shih tzu-liao ts'ung-k'an)*, published by Chien Po-tsan and others, Peking 1953, II, 177.

earth as possessing equal rights, just as in China during the second half of the last millenium B.C. a number of states with equal rights existed independently of each other. He seeks to see in the relations to each other of the states of China at that period an example for international relationship in the 19th century. He believes that proper principles for relations between states could be found in the *Spring and Autumn Annals* of Confucius, the subject of which is the history of that period. And thus he draws a parallel between the *Spring and Autumn Annals* and the international law of modern times. He believed that the Chinese government should follow its example and concern itself fully with foreign countries and international relations.

These ideas of the Reform Movement were not restricted to theoretical arguments. In spite of strong conservative opposition, there were increasing tendencies even within the government towards a change in the fundamental attitude to foreign nations and their rulers. From the very beginning of direct relations between China and the West (cf. Ch. III, §2 and V, §2 above) the question of the receiving of foreign envoys in audience by the Chinese Emperor had always been a source of controversy. The Chinese insisted on the traditional ceremonial, which to them was natural and obvious, including genuflections and the kotow on the part of foreigners; otherwise the audience was refused. Not until 1873, after long formal negotiations, was an audience accorded to an accredited foreign minister in Peking without the traditional ceremonial. Nevertheless, he was received not in the Inner Palace, but outside. The first similar audience after this took place in 1891. In 1894—actually on the initiative of the Chinese—the foreign ministers were invited for the first time to a magnificent audience in the Inner Palace, without the traditional ceremonial, on the occasion of the 60th birthday of the Empress Dowager Tz'u-hsi. In the same year, there followed, by imperial edict, the formal declaration of war upon Japan, as upon a state of equal standing. The traditional view only recognised punitive expeditions carried out at the command of a universal ruler against insubordinate barbarian tribes. When the brother of the German Emperor, Prince Heinrich, visited China in 1898, he was the first member of a foreign, Western ruling house to be received by the Empress Dowager and the Emperor in the Summer Palace Wan-shou-shan as a complete equal. Amongst other things, he went up on to the throne beside the Emperor to converse with him. The significance of this event can be clearly seen from the remark made to one of the foreign participants by Weng T'ung-ho, one of the senior statesmen who were present: 'We have experienced something un-exampled today, something for which there is no precedent in Chinese history'.[1]

The rejection of the traditional sinocentric point of view paved the way to modern nationalism, which held that China should use every means to defend her sovereignty against the foreign Powers, on the grounds that she possessed equal rights with them. To this end, fundamental reforms were necessary in every sphere. For this purpose, China had to learn from the West, just as in Chinese antiquity the individual states were not ashamed to learn from each other. Examples which were regarded as particularly relevant were the reforms of Peter the Great in Russia, and even more, those of the Meiji period in Japan, since 1868. Almost all suggestions for reforms inspired by Western originals were justified by reference to appropriate chapters and statements in the Canonical Writings. In a completely anachronistic way, interpretations were often foisted upon ancient texts which quite certainly could not have meant any such thing. These parallels, many of which were very forced, were not limited to the basic issues of the political and institutional structure, the democratisation of the government, morality, education, etc., but also included practical questions of economics, military tactics, school organisation, etc. Where the superiority of the West was obvious, a special attempt was always made to show, by citing the appropriate text, that similar ideas or institutions had already existed in Chinese

[1] Otto Franke, *Ostasiatische Neubildungen*, pp. 14–15; *Erinnerungen aus zwei Welten*, Berlin 1954, pp. 74–75, 100–102.

antiquity. It was suggested that for one reason or another these achievements had been neglected or forgotten in China, but more fully developed in the West. There was consequently every reason for China to go back to these original ideas and pick up the threads of their development again. In this way it was hoped to integrate Western civilisation, at least in theory, with the development of Chinese history. Here are a few examples of this procedure.

In an essay entitled *Studies on Parliaments in Ancient Times*, Liang Ch'i-ch'ao writes:

> . . . Is there any evidence for the existence of parliaments in [Chinese] antiquity? If we are looking for the example of the rulers of the early period, we must look for it in their ideas. Although the term "parliament" did not exist, there was something [corresponding] to this idea. In ancient times, in order to maintain the Universal Empire in harmony, the wise kings had recourse to the *Book of Changes*, [which reads]: "If high and low are in communication with one another, this is noble; if high and low are not in alliance with one another, this is wrong." In the *Book of Documents* we read: "All consult together"; and again, "Consult with the officials and with the people".
>
> In the *Book of Rites* we read: "It is the office of the *Hsiaosʐu-k'ou* to regulate the public audience, in order to let the people come together to consult: in the first place when the country is in danger, in the second place when the seat of government is moved, and thirdly at the inauguration of a prince".
>
> [The teaching], that one should be aided in coming to a decision by the mass of the people, and plan accordingly, is contained in the *Book of Rites*, where we read: "Keep in touch with the inhabitants of the country, and remain in confidence with them".—"To like what the people like and to detest what the people detest is to be father and mother of the people".—"To like what the people detest and to detest what the people like is to resist human feeling. Anyone who does this will certainly meet with evil."
>
> In Meng-tzu we read: "When the whole people says of someone that he is able, test this. When the whole people says of someone that he is worthless, test this [in the same way]. When the whole people says of someone that he should be killed, [test this. If it is found that it is in order to kill him], kill him." The Great Lords (*ch'ing shih*) in the "Great Plan" (*Hung-fan*) (in the *Book of Docu-*

ments) and the people of rank (*ta fu*) in Meng-tzu are the Upper House.

The masses in the "Great Plan" and the people in Meng-tzu are the Lower House. How can there be consultation except by means of these [institutions]? How else could there be communications [between the government and the people]? How could it be known what the people like and what they detest? Thus although the term "parliament" did not exist, its actual function did . . . [there follow further examples of a similar kind from the late Chou period and from the Ch'in and Han periods].

In the biography of Chu Po in the *Official History of the Han Period* we read, "[Chu] Po [who died in 5 B.C.] did not like the scholars to gather together, and simply removed the [institutions of the] meeting of officials to give advice with the words, 'How can one still make use of planning officials!' " Before this, officials had given advice in all provinces. In the states of the West, every country and every city has its advisory council, which has the same purpose.

The answer to the question as to when the parliaments of antiquity disappeared is that the parliaments formed a great hindrance to those who wished to corrupt the people. I do not know how many there were who following the arrogant example of Chu Po made it their desire to set aside these ancient institutions. As to whether one should re-introduce parliaments as soon as possible in order to strengthen China, the answer must be, "No!" An [appropriate] attitude must first spread throughout the whole country, literature and science must first flourish, and the level of education of the people must first be raised. Then parliaments can be set up. If the attempt was made to set up parliaments at the present day, this would lead to disorder. Thus parliaments form the foundation of a strong country. But schools form the foundation of parliaments.[1]

This essay by Liang Ch'i-ch'ao is characteristic of the arguments of progressive circles in the 1890s. Another author discusses the same theme under the title *On the Advantage of Introducing Popular Power in China*. He begins his analysis by referring to the same texts as Liang Ch'i-ch'ao and then continues:

Chinese who discuss governmental systems speak only in terms of governing the people by a ruler. In the West, however,

[1] *Huang Ch'ao ching-shih wen hsin-pien*, Book 5, 1, 16a–17b; quoted from W. Franke, 'Die staatspolitischen Reformversuche . . .' pp. 39–43.

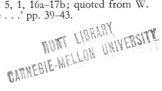

there are democratic countries and also countries governed jointly by the ruler and the people. Chinese scholars are surprised and consider it strange. Nevertheless what is strange about it? In ancient times all who discussed government always gave consideration to the people below. Thus the chapter "Hung-fan" of the Book of History says "to deliberate with the common people", and the chapter "Lü-hsing" says, "The emperor frankly consults the people below him". In the Rites of Chou it is stated that the official in charge of the provincial administration brought the multitude of people together to ask their opinion. . . . Mencius says, "When the people of the nation unanimously say that someone is capable, then he may be employed; when the people of the nation unanimously say that he is incapable, then he may be removed; and when the people of the nation unanimously say that he may be killed, then kill him". Other such references appearing in the classics are too numerous to be counted on the fingers. This shows that in ancient times those who governed the nation were not without the desire to govern it together with the people. . . .[1]

In the *Admonitions for Study* of Chang Chih-tung a special chapter is devoted to the uniting and integration of traditional Chinese and modern Western knowledge. One passage reads:

. . . In the [Book of] the *Doctrine of the Mean* we read: "Whoever possesses the greatest sincerity in the world, can penetrate the nature of things and expedite the transformations that take place in heaven and on earth". This is the meaning of natural science as taught in the West.

In the *Rites of Chou* [we read of] methods of bringing about soil changes, means for improving silk and hemp, and for transforming the eight basic materials. This is the purpose of chemistry. . . . In the *Analects* [of Confucius] we read, "The craftsman sharpens his tools"; or in the *Book of Documents*, "[The craftsmen] does not look for old tools, but for new." This means that industry should use modern machines. . . .[2]

These examples are sufficient to show the characteristic attitude of the champions of the Reform Movement to Western

---

[1] *Wu-hsü pien-fa* . . . *tzu-liao* III, 147; In Teng-Fairbank, *China's Response to the West*, p. 161; W. Franke, 'Reformversuche . . . .' p. 43–44.

[2] Jérome Tobar, *Chang Chih-tung, K'iuen-hio p'ien*, Shanghai 1909, pp. 176–177; In W. Franke, 'Reformversuche . . .' p. 18–19.

civilisation. It displays a revolutionary advance by contrast with the period from the Opium War up to the 1880s. Traditional conceptions are beginning to decline, although they still largely decide the mode of thought.

The religious propaganda of Christianity put forward by the foreign missionaries provoked a particular reaction from K'ang Yu-wei and other exponents of the Reform Movement. Recognising the deficiencies of Confucianism purely as a religious doctrine—which of course it was never intended to be —they sought to compensate for this, in association with the unorthodox New Text School of Confucianism, which built on the Kungyang commentary to the *Spring and Autumn Annals*. They suggested that Confucius should hold a similar position to the Christian God, and that the Canonical Writings should be regarded as sacred in the same way as the Christian Bible, and read aloud in religious ceremonies, like Christian services, and interpreted in sermons. In the same way, a special religious category (*tao k'o*) should be incorporated into the state examinations. Those who took these examinations, like theologians in the Christian Churches of the West, should take on the rôle of clergy and act as priests and even as missionaries of Confucianism both in China and abroad. On the one hand, the Reform Movement played an essential part in breaking up Confucianism as a political and social system, with its own distinctive and unified basis on the secular and intellectual plane. To replace it, they attempted to salvage part of this system from the inevitable collapse, and set it up on its own. They wanted to turn Confucianism into a religion separated from the political and social system, on the pattern of Christianity. Those who advanced this idea did not perceive that the part to which they wished to give an independent existence rested upon the same basis as Confucianism as a whole. It was as though they were trying to decorate the roof of a house of which they were at the same time demolishing the foundations. All attempts to salvage Confucianism as a closed system of doctrine in the form of a religion, once the traditional state had collapsed, were ultimately in vain. Only a few individual elements of Confucian teaching later continued to play their part, as they do even today.

3. THE ABOLITION OF THE TRADITIONAL CHINESE EXAMINATION SYSTEM AND THE OPENING OF THE EDUCATIONAL SYSTEM TO WESTERN CULTURE

The essay of Liang Ch'i-ch'ao quoted above, which in other respects is not very convincing, pointed very accurately at the end to the fact that an essential prerequisite for a changed attitude to modern politics and science, based on Western civilisation, was an appropriate educational formation. Thus a fundamental question in all reforms was that of the incorporation of certain elements of Western education into the Chinese system of education and training. From the elementary stage on this was directed towards the state examinations, which were the entry to the privileged *Shen-shih* class and to officialdom. The content of the examinations was almost exclusively the Confucian teaching in the orthodox interpretation of Chu Hsi (1130–1200), which had been universally accepted since the 15th century. What was known as the 'eight-legged essay', to be written in a very formalist manner on a theme from the 'Four Books', a group of the Canonical Writings, formed the nucleus of every examination. In spite of every well-founded criticism, the 'eight-legged essay' was the principal factor in the centuries that followed in deciding the result and the outcome of the examination. From childhood on, the whole of one's studies were normally concentrated on learning in a more or less mechanical way the art of writing such 'eight-legged essays'. It was inevitable that a literary education of such a formalist nature was bound to have an extremely limiting and ossifying effect on the intellectual agility of the whole educated class in China, which of course was the ruling class. Only a few individuals succeeded in breaking out of this intellectual strait-jacket and recognising the evil effects of such formalised examinations.

The Opium War and the increasing oppression of China

which followed it provided a new stimulus for criticism of the content of the state examinations. Up to the last decade of the century, however, the criticial arguments that were brought to bear still did not manifest any essential influence from Western ideas or institutions. Basically they followed the same course as in the previous centuries. In the 1870s a few more far-seeing personalities amongst the higher officials began by attempting to introduce mathematics or even 'foreign subjects' *(yang wu)* as a supplementary category in addition to the literary examination. But all these attempts came to grief against the resistance of 'public opinion', in the sense described above, which it was so easy to mobilise against all novelty, at court and in the government. Nevertheless, from the 1860s on, direct practical needs had led to the foundation of a series of military, technical and language schools. The view gained increasing acceptance that a degree of schooling in modern 'Western' scientific and intellectual pursuits was indispensable for the maintenance of the traditional Chinese state. But the progress of these few modern schools was not particularly encouraging, for the successful completion of their courses did not lead to the granting of a literary degree nor, in consequence, to the social prestige and corresponding privileges associated with it. Who was prepared to devote himself to a study that could not lead to office and rank, which was the goal for which every Chinese was striving?

Here we come to the central problem about which the conflict with Western civilization chiefly revolved after the end of the last century. For the main point at issue in this conflict was the educational system. A vicious circle resulted which proved only too difficult to break: in order to preserve the traditional state, it was necessary that officials should be educated in modern Western subjects. In order to bring about a serious study of these new subjects, and to obtain officials educated in them, they had somehow to be incorporated into the examination system. But by the acceptance of Western subjects into the examinations, the exclusiveness of Confucian education would be broken down, and the unified ideological basis of the prevailing political and social doctrine would be open to question. But to abandon the indoctrination of the Confucian ideology was bound seriously to threaten the existence of the traditional state and could—as in fact was later the case—lead to its collapse.

From 1898 on, various attempts were undertaken to reform the examination system by the introduction of new material and by associating it with the schools of modern studies. Finally, in 1904, the complete integration of the schools' examinations with the state examinations and the gradual abolition of the old style of literary examination was decreed. Nevertheless, the majority of scholars did not yet seem to be convinced that this was a definitive and irrevocable measure. Most of them still regarded the old traditional way as the simplest and safest; the new schools failed to establish themselves, and the urgently needed new generation of officials trained in modern subjects was lacking as before. In 1905 this caused six of the highest officials to bring their influence to bear in common and to propose the immediate abolition of the traditional system. The proposal was accepted, and thus the traditional examination system was finally brought to an end. In theory, in fact, the old examination grades remained unaltered, but henceforth could only be gained by success in the final examinations in the appropriate schools. In these schools modern knowledge was taught on the same level as the traditional learning. But it soon became clear that once the traditional system had been given up, there was little justification for continuing to bestow the old degrees; amongst other things, the restriction on the number of successful examination candidates, which had been fundamental to the earlier system, had also been abandoned. The old forms were inadequate to their new content. This new content ultimately brought down not only the old forms of education, but in the revolution of 1911 destroyed the whole structure of the traditional state which had enshrined these forms.

Only after the examination had been removed was the door really opened in China to modern scientific and intellectual studies and to political and social ideas from the West. Instead of a largely passive resistance, increasingly difficult to maintain, to Western ideas, there now began an active encounter with Western civilisation. Thus the year 1905, when the examination system was abolished, represents a decisive turning point in the relationship of China to the West in the intellectual and cultural fields.

4. A New Evaluation of the West: The May Fourth Movement of 1919

After the Chinese educational system had been opened to Western culture and civilisation by the abolition of the examination system in 1905, the overthrow of the traditional political structure in the revolution of 1911 provided the necessary political conditions for a new attitude to the West and to Western culture. But this did not come to fruition until a few years later in the Chinese cultural revolution, the visible expression of which was the May Fourth Movement of 1919. Its name is taken from the great demonstration of protest which the students of Peking staged on that day against the signing of the Paris Peace Treaty. This treaty provided for the transfer of the former German Protectorate of Kiachou, and all previous German rights in the Shantung province, to Japan. The students energetically demanded that China's claim should be taken into account; their action was followed by further expressions of protest throughout the country, accompanied by strikes on the part of workers and business employees in the new economic centres, and by the boycott of Japanese goods. As a result, the Government, which was friendly towards Japan, found itself obliged to give way to the pressure of public opinion, and the Chinese representatives at the Peace Conference were instructed to refuse to sign the treaty.

But these were only the outward events. Behind them was a great revolutionary movement for the cultural renewal of China. It was principally directed against the social and moral norms which had come down from the past, and which still prevailed in spite of the breakdown of the traditional system, and against the traditionally oriented thinking of the government and the leading political groups. These were still guided by the traditional pattern of life and ideas of Confucianism. At first, the attack of the new intelligentsia upon Confucianism was largely based on an appeal to its opponents in China's past. But it did not limit itself to these traditional Chinese elements. It was increasingly recognised that Confucianism was inseparably linked with the monarchy and irreconcilable with the Republic. But they went even further. A total break with the whole of Chinese tradition, and the adoption of Western culture and civilisation, seemed to many of the radical leaders of the May Fourth Movement to be the only way of salvation for China. What was meant by Western culture in these circles was a mixture of Western ideas and achievements from the period since the 18th century. They held in particularly high regard the ideas that came from the French and the American revolutions. 'Democracy' and 'Science'—sometimes referred to as 'Mr. Democracy' and 'Mr. Science'—were their guiding concepts. To them, these concepts seemed to embody the activity and vitality of the West and its superiority over China. Their conception of 'democracy' was taken from the liberalism of the Manchester School; they regarded its goal as the freeing of the individual from all the limits imposed by traditional restraints. They believed that the individual, freed from all bonds, would then achieve the same success in China as in the West. By 'science' they meant simply a method to achieve material progress, and above all a means of struggling against 'superstition'. And they termed every religious belief without exception 'superstition'. They believed that 'science' —as they understood it—should serve to break down the traditional social order, based as it was on certain fundamental religious concepts; science should help to overcome Confucianism, as well as every other religious doctrine and every other tradition based on religious concepts. This anti-traditionalism on the one hand, associated with an uncritical, superficial admiration of Western patterns of government and society on the other hand, were characteristic of most members of the progressive Chinese intelligentsia at that period, and to a considerable degree have remained so since. Thus within a few decades the Chinese attitude to the West and to its culture changed from one extreme to the other.

The May Fourth Movement brought with it a complete re-orientation of Chinese thought. An as example of this new attitude we quote the words written at the end of 1918 by the President of the University of Peking Ts'ai Yüan-p'ei (1867–1940):

> What is called a university is not merely a place for a majority of the students to attend classes on time and to be furnished with the qualifications for becoming graduates. It is actually an organ-ization for academic research by professors and students working together. By research we mean not merely the learning about European culture, but also the necessity of making further discoveries on the basis of European culture; it is not merely for preservation of the essentials of our national culture (*kuo-ts'ui*), it is also necessary to use scientific methods to expound the real nature of our national essentials.[1]

These words show very clearly the fundamentally new point of view from which the cultures of China and the West were seen in their relative significance. China, with her intellectual and cultural life, now began to take part in that of the rest of the world, even though at first she received more than she gave.

From a vague and often superficial knowledge of the new Western ideas, it was easy at first to form a united front against tradition on the basis of a few leading concepts. But this unity was destroyed in proportion as the whole complex of Western thought was more profoundly studied, and the Chinese students became more conscious of the variety and frequent contra-diction of the basic principles that underlay it. Thus there were soon sharp controversies between Chinese representatives of conflicting Western ideas. All the great intellectual currents of the Western world began to manifest themselves in China and

[1] Quoted from Teng-Fairbank, *China's Response to the West*, p. 238.

I

to find their exponents there. Very soon, the original unity of the May Fourth Movement broke up into two main tendencies, the liberal-democratic on the one hand and the Communist on the other. The example looked to by the first, as a result of the ever more intensive American cultural propaganda, tended to be the United States and the American way of life. For example, the lectures given by the American philosopher John Dewey in the years 1919–20 as the guest of the University of Peking, and elsewhere in China, left behind an extraordinarily powerful impression. Dewey's positivistic thought, directed towards the practical problems of life, possessed a great appeal for the Chinese academics. Thus in bidding farewell to Dewey from Peking in July 1921, Hu Shih (1891–1962) wrote:

> We may say that since China has come into contact with Western civilisation, no foreign scholar has had so great an effect upon the intellectual world of China as Mr. Dewey. And we may add that in the decades to come there will be no other foreign scholar whose effect in China will be greater than that of Mr. Dewey.[1]

And in 1926 Hu Shih praised Western civilisation in the highest terms. After he had rejected the criticism that European civilisation is purely materialistic, by contrast to the spiritual civilisation of the East, he wrote:

> Such a civilisation, making rich use of the intelligence and knowledge of man in striving for truth, in order to set free the spirit of man, which subdues the workings of nature to itself, in order to place them at man's service, which transforms its material environment in order to give a new shape to the social and political system, and which is concerned for the greatest happiness of the greatest number of men—such a civilisation should be able to satisfy the spiritual claims of mankind; it is a spiritual civilisation, a truly idealistic civilisation, and certainly not a materialistic civilisation.[2]

At first, Marxism was little noticed in China. This was not

---

[1] Quoted from W. Franke, *Chinas kulturelle Revolution. Die Bewegung vom 4. Mai 1919*, Munich, 1957, p. 51.
[2] *Hu Shih wen-ts'un* III, ch. 1, p. 21.

because its thinking was felt to be too extreme; for it was the newest and most radical idea of the West which exercised a particular attraction on the open-minded Chinese intelligentsia of that period. But in its original form, the teaching of Marx was relevant to a highly industrialised society, and seemed to be of no significance for China. It was only after the October Revolution in Russia that Marxism, in the interpretation and dogmatic form given to it by Lenin, began to claim attention in China. It was realised that the Communist teaching could be applied even to a country which was economically scarcely less backward than China. In addition, the Comintern immediately proclaimed as an important item in its programme the liberation of the colonial and semi-colonial nations from the yoke of the Imperial Powers. Simultaneously, the new Soviet government renounced all previous privileges and rights possessed by Czarist Russia in China. Consequently, Soviet Russia became the first Western nation voluntarily to accord to China the equal rights she had sought for so long. Thus wide circles in China began to look to the Soviet Union as the friend and champion of the oppressed nations in their struggle for freedom and equal rights. A group of leading personalities in the May Fourth Movement went further than this in accepting the messianic message of the Russian revolution, and founded the Communist Party of China in 1921 (according to to other sources 1920).

The liberal-democratic groups, looking to the U.S.A., and the Communists, their hopes directed towards the Soviet Union, were only the two extreme wings of those in China who came most strongly under the influence of the West. A large number of them stood between these extremes, closer to one or the other of the two sides. And the degree to which individuals were willing to accept Western ideas and Western cultural achievements varied extraordinarily. Furthermore, the growing scepticism of that period towards Western civilisation also found its adherents in China. Thus Liang Ch'i-ch'ao, at first one of the most zealous admirers of Western culture, wrote after his journey to Europe in 1919:

Those who praised the omnipotence of science had hoped previously that, as soon as science succeeded, the golden age would appear forthwith. Now science is successful indeed; material progress in the West in the last one hundred years has greatly surpassed the achievements of the three thousand years prior to this period. Yet we human beings have not secured happiness; on the contrary, science gives us catastrophes. We are like travellers losing their way in a desert. They see a big black shadow ahead, and desperately run to it, thinking that it may lead them somewhere. But after running a long way, they no longer see the shadow and fall into the slough of despond. What is that shadow? It is this "Mr. Science".[1]

The educated classes of China in the 1920s and 1930s displayed every shade of opinion between total rejection of everything from the West, and the advocacy of complete Westernisation. This of course is true only of their conscious attitudes to Western culture and civilisation. Even those Chinese who most ardently demanded Westernisation in one sense or another were as a rule unconsciously more or less influenced by traditional Chinese habits of thought. And those who categorically rejected any Westernisation were only very rarely able to avoid completely the effects of modern ideas and conceptions drawn from the West. Thus the May Fourth Movement signifies for China's attitude to the West the defeat of a way of thought exclusively centred on China, and her entry as a conscious and active participant into the intellectual and political conflicts which at that period preoccupied the whole world.

5. THE SPECIAL STATUS OF WESTERNERS IN CHINA AND ITS EFFECTS ON THE CHINESE

China, of course, never came under the direct rule of a Western state as a colony. Yet there was justification for the remark of Sun Yat-sen that it was a 'hyper-colony', everybody's colony. All the Western nations felt that they were united

[1] *Yin-ping-shih ho-chi*, Book 21, ch. 23, p. 12. Cf. also Chow Tse-tsung, *The May Fourth Movement*, Cambridge, Mass. 1960, p. 328.

there as a colonial power, and had assured a privileged position for their own nationals through the 'unequal treaties'. But even after the end of the 1920s, when the Nationalist government of the Kuomintang had made considerable progress in obtaining the according of equal rights to China—it was in fact not until after 1943 that the last remnants of the 'unequal treaties' disappeared—elements of the colonialism of the past still remained in the attitude of foreigners in China, as individuals or as a group. This can be seen from the examples that follow.

Even into the 1920s the Chinese could not enter certain restaurants in some foreign settlements, and could not travel first-class on the trams; a park in Shanghai was forbidden to 'dogs and Chinese'. In the international clubs of many cities the Chinese were specifically excluded right up to the second World War. When in the spring of 1949, after the occupation of North China by the Communists, the sea route between Tientsin and Hong Kong was reopened by a British shipping firm, they continued the regulation that had been normal in foreign coasters, that no first-class passages were sold to the Chinese. This discrimination was only abandoned after an energetic protest by the new Communist government. In Peking, up to the time of the occupation of the city by the Japanese in 1937, only the foreign personnel of foreign embassies had the legal right to go on to the platform at the station without a platform ticket, but in practice this right was exercised by every foreigner. The Chinese had to buy a platform ticket. Foreigners needed no number plate on their bicycles. All other bicycles had to have one. At the numerous police cordons and investigations on the streets and stations outside the foreign settlements, foreigners, even when like the Germans they no longer possessed the right of extra-territoriality, used to pass through unmolested, right up to the last war. They accepted this preferential treatment not as a special act of politeness towards foreign guests, but as a natural privilege. The foreigner felt himself to be a colonial overlord, just as in the Asiatic and African colonies of the

Great Powers. As we have already mentioned (cf. Ch. V, §4 above) there was an extraordinary difference in the treatment of foreign and native Chinese employees, not only in the foreign settlements but throughout China. It is true that a foreigner inexperienced in Chinese ways needed a much higher sum than a Chinese to obtain the same purchasing power. But the basic difference in salaries went far beyond what was customary in other countries to make up this discrepancy in purchasing power, as well as certain additional needs of a foreigner unused to the native climatic and other conditions. For what counted here was not qualification or skill; rather, the foreigner belonged on principle, without regard to his personal ability or the service he provided, to a higher category than the Chinese. This point of view, with the resulting inequality in the payment of employees by foreign firms, persisted with certain limitations even beyond the end of the second World War.

The Chinese are mostly very sensitive to actual power and property relations. Simple men without education often accepted these distinctions as something given by destiny, and as a result were not consumed by envy and jealousy. It is also a fact that in spite of the basic discrimination that was there, many Chinese often worked in foreign businesses under more favourable conditions than in many purely Chinese enterprises. The reaction of the educated classes, however, was different. Their traditional contempt, rooted in their pride in their own civilisation, for the Westerners who had burst into China with brutal force, had been replaced by nationalist ideas drawn from an education strongly influenced by the West. For them, the idea, constantly proclaimed by the West, of the fundamental equality of all men and nations, showed up the inequality that actually existed in an even more glaring light. This inequality was defended by the Westerners with extreme tenacity, and was bound to give rise to most unfriendly feelings towards the West on the part of the educated Chinese. But there were other factors which increased this anti-Western feeling.

Since the middle of the previous century, the foreigners,

and not least the missionaries, had begun, consciously or unconsciously, to corrode away the traditional religion and morality, and also the long established social structure of China, by spreading Western ideas and the Western way of life. It is true that this process was inevitable. But it is easy to gauge the bitter feelings against those who caused it, which this process of corrosion was bound to arouse amongst those classes in China who were conscious of their civilisation and traditions. These feelings have persisted down to the present day, even though in the meantime the same classes have long recognised that the traditional order could not be maintained, and are themselves eager to replace it (cf. §4 above). An individual can scarcely be thankful to someone who has destroyed his faith and his ideals; instead, he is angry and hates him. The same is true of a whole people. In the last hundred years it has been rare for Westerners to adapt themselves completely to the traditional Chinese way of life. An exception is very impressively described by Nora Waln in her book *The House of Exile*. As a rule, the foreigners, including most missionaries, not only maintained their own Western way of life and looked down arrogantly upon the Chinese, but they also sought as far as possible to spread their customs and standards amongst those around them. The influence of the American Protestant missionaries in this direction was very powerful. As a rule, the aim of their missionary work was not merely the propagation of the Christian religion, but also of the American way of life. They were impelled by the honest conviction that America quite simply represented the progress and upward development of mankind in an absolute and universally valid form. America was called to lead other backward nations along the path of American democracy and the American spirit of progress, to a better future. By their personal example, by the spoken and written word, and by the use of films, American missionaries— mostly without the slightest real understanding of and insight into Chinese realities—sought to propagate a foreign ideal of life which was not understood, and which in the circumstances of China had a destructive rather than a constructive effect.

In addition to the Americans, other nations also carried out this cultural propaganda to a lesser degree, again mostly through missionaries. They concentrated above all on education. There was only a small proportion of the whole of the population of China who went to school at all, and an even smaller number who went to a middle school or followed any kind of advanced course. This educated élite occupied most of the leading positions in the state and in society. Thus their relationship to the foreigners was of particular importance.

As we have described above (Ch. V, §3), from the beginning of the 20th century on the foreign missions began to maintain an increasing number of schools of every kind. At first, they were mostly reserved exclusively for Christian pupils and students. But they were soon opened to all. Thus the mission schools became a predominant factor in the spread of Western ideas and the Western way of life, and formed the centre of what is known in Communist terminology as the 'cultural invasion'. Up to the 1920s, in fact, instruction in the mission schools was mostly conducted according to the system of the country from which the missionaries came, and in the language of that country. The peculiarly Chinese branches of knowledge —Chinese language, literature, history, geography, etc.—were often given very scanty treatment. The control of the schools lay for the most part in foreign hands. The part played by Chinese was often only a subordinate one. More and more, this situation began to be regarded as intolerable by the Chinese not only outside the mission schools, but also within them. For it was in these very schools that they learned the concepts of national self-determination and democracy. Thus after the Nationalist government of the Kuomintang had come to power at the end of the 1920s, it emphatically insisted, in spite of all resistance on the part of foreign missionaries and every protest by foreign governments, on the demand for Chinese sovereignty in all educational matters. The mission school had to come under the control of the Chinese education authorities and follow the Chinese curriculum, abandon obligatory instruction in the Christian religion for all pupils, appoint a Chinese as the responsible headmaster, etc.

It is true that in spite of this there continued to be extensive foreign influence in the Chinese education system. The Chinese headmaster was often no more than a figurehead; for the foreigners controlled the money. Foreign educational institutions were for the most part better situated financially and better equipped than those which were entirely Chinese. They were often better organised and offered a better education. In the 1930s some mission universities attained a leading position not only in medicine, natural science and Western languages, but actually in the sphere of Chinese studies. At the same time, particularly in the light of events since 1948, it may well be asked whether their effect was not in the end more negative than positive.

The reason for this is that in China secondary schools and colleges are for the most part boarding institutions. Thus they have a considerable effect on the formation of character, and sometimes it is easy to tell the college at which a certain Chinese academic was educated. The mission schools only rarely succeeded in producing an open and generous personality of firm convictions. The prevailing atmosphere in the mission schools was formed by the superiority of the foreigners. Not only did the foreigners provide the money, thus holding the whip hand in all internal matters in the school; without for the most part being conscious of it, they imposed by their way of life a heavy burden on young Chinese, who being at an impressionable stage in their development, were inevitably given the feeling that they were fundamentally second class personalities. Even after the second World War, at many mission universities a missionary working as a university teacher received more 'han twenty times the salary of his Chinese colleague. The latter may very well have obtained a far better education and qualification abroad than the missionary himself. Even a foreign female secretary in the university office could sometimes receive more than ten times the salary of a Chinese professor. In many universities the foreigners lived in large and beautiful houses with numerous servants, while the Chinese lecturers lived for the most part in small and sometimes wretched huts on the same campus. It is true that many missionaries gave away much money for charitable purposes, and that many of them kept open house not only for the Christians of their own mission. But this could not remove the fundamental difference in the status of missionaries and native Chinese employees. This discrimination produced either envy and jealousy—often unexpressed—or a powerful feeling of inferiority, which was often expressed in a lack of personal initiative and a servile dependence upon the foreigners. It often led to powerful expressions of resentment. It is characteristic that when the mission schools were taken over by the Communists, and the foreigners were discriminated against, the Chinese who showed themselves most loyal to the foreigners were often those who were not Christians, who had preserved their personal independence, and who had previously often come into sharp conflict with the foreigners.

The effect of the mission schools on those outside them was also harmful to them in the long run. One cannot speak of a discrimination against the mission schools and their pupils and students, or a general contempt for them. But the pupils and students of the leading secondary schools and colleges that were entirely Chinese liked to look down a little on the mission schools and their fellow students there. The latter often tended to display foreign habits in their outward behaviour. Teachers and lecturers often preferred to work at purely Chinese institutions. In spite of this, the better conditions offered by the mission schools often made it possible for them to attract good teaching staff. But those outside the mission schools had no opportunity of becoming acquainted with the positive side of the foreigners who worked there, and thus they frequently regarded them as nothing more than the representatives of an unwanted 'cultural invasion'. Besides this, in their home countries, in order to raise funds for their work in China, the missionaries tended to describe in their words, their writings and their photographs the misery, poverty and lack of education there. Consequently, an extremely one-sided view of China was propagated. This greatly embittered many Chinese who learnt of it. It is true that all these unfortunate features were present to an immense degree; but they only formed one aspect of the matter, and the Chinese were particularly sensitive about it.

Many missionaries and other foreigners did outstanding work in their own sphere of activity in China. Many behaved personally in exemplary fashion and consequently won affection and respect within the narrow Chinese circles in which they moved. But this was not sufficient to overcome the universal resentment against the foreigners as privileged colonial masters. In fact the ability and achievements of foreigners, surpassing those of many Chinese, were the last things to win them unreserved affection. On the contrary, they often had the opposite effect, especially amongst the educated classes. Objective admiration and recognition of the achievements of the foreigners were often mingled with a subjective feeling of envy and jealousy. Furthermore, the missionaries, filled with the consciousness of the higher level of their civilisation, their religion and their morality, did not always maintain the necessary discretion with regard to Chinese customs and feelings. By the friendly compassion with which they looked down upon the 'heathen' they often provoked more ill-will on the part of those Chinese who were conscious of their national civilisation and culture, than the merchants in the ports, who mostly lived their own lives amongst themselves and had little contact with such Chinese.

6.   THE ANTI-IMPERIALIST AND ANTI-CHRISTIAN MOVEMENT

In the previous sections we have summed up the reasons which provoked widespread bitterness and hostility amongst the Chinese against the West and its representatives in China. This bitterness, stirred up time and again during the past century, has repeatedly manifested itself in a series of violent outbreaks (cf. Ch. 5, §3 above). Until about the end of the last century it was mainly conservative circles in the *Shen-shih* class who were the champions of active resistance against the foreigners. The revolutionary movement which grew with increasing rapidity from that time on considered that the main blame for China's misfortune lay with the ruling Manchu dynasty and the traditional political system. In their struggle against this, the revolutionaries tried to learn and even to draw support from the West. It is true that the revolutionaries under the leadership of Sun Yat-sen felt most strongly the humiliations and the wrongs that China had had to suffer from the foreign Powers. Nevertheless, they felt that the ruling Manchu régime had provoked such treatment by its inflexible and reactionary policies. To the extent to which the structure of the Chinese state and its government adapted itself to the demands of the time, the foreigners would gradually make a voluntary renunciation of the 'unequal treaties' and the privileges that came from them. Even after the fall of the dynasty and the founding of the Republic in 1911, Sun Yat-sen based his plans for the reconstruction of the country on generous political and economic support by the West, in order to change China into a modern state. The attitude of the Powers during the next stages of the development, especially in Paris in 1919 and in Washington in 1921–22, soon cured Sun Yat-sen and his followers of their illusions. It was obvious that the Powers had never dreamt of the independent political and economic development of China, nor of the voluntary renunciation of any of the privileges they had obtained from the 'unequal treaties'. The attitude of Soviet Russia, on the other hand, was quite different. Its government did not merely plead in theoretical terms for the liberation of the Asian nations from Western colonial rule and imperialism, but took the practical step of renouncing all the privileges which the Czarist régime had possessed in China, such as the right of extra-territoriality and the Russian settlements in a number of ports. The Russian Orthodox mission had never played any significant rôle. Thus the new Russia seemed to many to be China's obvious ally in the struggle against Western and Japanese hegemony.

The first great anti-imperialist movement occurred in the years 1925–27. It was directed principally against Britain. Its most effective weapon was that of the boycott. This involved not only British goods and ships, but also a considerable proportion of the Chinese workers and employees of British businesses in the British settlement in Canton and the nearby colony of Hong Kong, so that even domestic servants employed by British households left their place of work. The boycott continued unremittingly for more than a year, and seriously damaged the British China trade. In many places there were violent clashes which increased the tension. Soon after the Nationalist government had moved from Canton to Wuhan in 1926, the Chinese populace there forced their way into the British concession and demanded its return to China. Thanks to the wisdom of the government in London, which by no means corresponded to the wishes of the 'old China hands', this did not result in any significant incident. A short time afterwards the British concession in Kiukiang was taken back by the Chinese in a similar way. As a precaution all British subjects, mostly missionaries and merchants, were evacuated from the inland regions. Most British women and children also left the British settlements in the treaty ports.

The anti-Christian movement was closely linked to the anti-imperialist movement. During the advance of the revolutionary army in the years 1926–27, mission property was plundered and attacks were made repeatedly on foreign missionaries. It is true that in this context the anti-Christian movement is scarcely to be distinguished from the anti-imperialist movement. It was directed in the first place against the Anglo-Saxon missions, which for practical purposes meant the Protestant missions, which were mostly in the hands of British and American missionaries. In the course of the evacuation of Southern China, more than two thousand missionaries, mostly British and American, left the country. Since the beginning of the 1920s the progressive revolutionary elements, especially pupils at school and students, had taken the lead in the struggle against the foreign missions. Most of them made no distinction between the Christian religion and those who propagated it. The struggle against the missionaries amounted to a struggle against Christianity. In addition to these nationalist, anti-colonial and anti-imperialist motives, there were other factors at work to a lesser degree. Prominent amongst these were the new ideas of the May Fourth Movement (cf. §4 above); most of its adherents sought to abolish Christianity in particular and religion in general, as out of date, unprogressive, unscientific and as 'superstition'. Religion was simply irreconcilable with the naïve belief in progress held by most members of the May Fourth Movement. In this attitude, the new intelligentsia had unconsciously adopted a legacy of the system of thought of the Confucian scholars, which was exclusively centred upon this world.

After the Nationalist government of the Kuomintang had been recognised in 1927, it energetically continued the struggle it had begun in the period of the revolution against the 'unequal treaties' and foreign privileges. As early as 1928 it succeeded in concluding treaties with a number of Powers on the basis of fundamentally equal recognition. Several countries such as Belgium, Denmark, Italy, Portugal and Spain gave up the right of extra-territoriality for their subjects in China from the 1st January, 1930. Germany had already had to give up all essential privileges in China in the Paris Peace Treaty, which was not signed by China, and ratified this renunciation in the German-Chinese Peace Treaty of 1921. Germany was not the loser by this action. It is true that the Great Powers still retained a number of fundamental privileges. But in the decade 1927–1937 the Nationalist government succeeded, in the course of negotiations for the recovery of foreign settlements in a number of treaty ports and of the British leased territory of Weihaiwei. In addition it obtained certain concessions with regard to the customs tariff, and the prospect of the renunciation of other foreign privileges. It was the second World War which eventually caused the Powers to renounce their last privileges. As one of the 'four Great Powers', along with the U.S.A., Britain and Russia, China finally achieved the status of complete international equality.

Thus after the war the 'unequal treaties' belonged to the past. China had regained her full sovereignty and the greater part of the territories leased or ceded since the 1890s. If the war had not created conditions of chaos in China, but had made possible the peaceful development of the country and its inhabitants, and the gradual evaluation of the new situation, the passage of time might perhaps have brought with it a restoration of the balance and a return to normal in the relationship between the Westerners and the native Chinese, such as seems to be developing, for example, in India and in some other former colonial areas. But the bitterness and humiliations of the past, the resentment at the privileged position of the foreigners, which was taking so long to over-throw, and which had been built up over generations and become habitual, were still so powerful at the end of the 1940s that it was not difficult for Communist propaganda to make use of these emotions. The Japanese had already regarded themselves from the very beginning of the War as the liberators of China, as of the whole of East and South-East Asia, from Western imperialism, and had tried to stir up Chinese feeling against the West. They demonstrated to the Chinese how it was possible to discriminate against individual Westerners in China and to harass them. Of course it was plainly obvious to every Chinese that Western imperialism had been replaced by a brutal Japanese imperialism which was much more oppressive to individuals. At that period, Europeans and Americans in Japanese-occupied China enjoyed a sympathy they had scarcely ever known. But the effect of the Japanese propaganda was that a few years later the anti-imperialist statements of the Communists were nothing new to the inhabitants of the occupied areas. But this time they fell on fruitful ground.

Characteristic of the atmosphere of tension after the war was the extraordinary agitation throughout China, when during Christmas 1946 in Peking a Chinese girl student was allegedly raped by an American soldier. In spite of the fact that the Americans had liberated China from the Japanese, that American troops were stationed in the country at the express wish of the Chinese government until the repatriation of all Japanese troops was concluded, and that, furthermore, actual assaults on women by Chinese soldiers within China were no rarity, a powerful surge of anti-American feeling was manifested everywhere in the shape of newspaper articles, student demonstrations, pamphlets, etc. Even many otherwise peaceful and thoughtful Chinese were seized by it. It is true that the Communists, who were particularly active at that period amongst students, were glad to take advantage of such an incident. But the universal outcry was spontaneous at first. The attitude of the numerous circles in China towards the West, and especially towards the United States, which was to say the least very critical, was displayed in other occurrences besides this, before the victory of the Communists. Even before 1948, the officials of the Nationalist government often liked to let foreigners feel the weight of Chinese authority, and to show them that the Chinese were now masters in their own country. In spite of the help and support that China had received, sympathy for the Americans increasingly declined, even in the Kuomintang and the groups associated with it. Even during the war, the incomparably better equipment and supplies of the American troops fighting the Japanese as allies of the Chinese, as well as the high claims of the American soldiers and their limited ability by comparison with the Chinese to suffer deprivations, had not always served to make the Americans particularly popular with the Chinese troops. Criticism of the corruption, incompetence and deficient ability of the Chinese military leaders, which was in most cases perfectly justified, but was not always very tactfully expressed by the Americans, gave rise to a great deal of bad blood. Thus in the critical years of the struggle with the Communists following the capitulation of Japan, feeling towards the United States in the Nationalist Army was not altogether friendly. The American policy in the middle of the 1940s, which was one of mediation between the Communists and the Nationalist government, but which was ultimately without success, provoked violent criticism in China from both sides. Thus by 1948, when the Communists seized power, the general attitude to America was by no means positive, but was widely critical, if not entirely negative.

This largely emotional attitude towards America and the West made it on the whole very easy for the Communists to work skilfully with their propaganda on the anti-Western attitude that had already existed, to provide an apparent justification for their drastic discriminatory measures. In the years which followed 1949 virtually all foreigners were expelled from the country, if they did not leave voluntarily. Many were arrested and condemned for real or alleged offences against Chinese laws, sometimes in show trials, but for the most part with the public excluded. The legal proceedings and trials were carried out in a way which was not only customary in other Communist countries, but which had been in use for many centuries in China, especially in periods of disturbance. According to traditional Chinese legal custom, no one could be condemned without a confession. Thus abuses of all kinds had often been used to obtain confessions. After a political revolution, the victorious ruling party had often rid itself of its opponents by forcing them to sign 'confessions' of high treason drawn up by the new government, on the basis of which they could be condemned according to the law. By insisting on consular jurisdiction for their subjects, the Western Powers had tried to protect them from this kind of trial, and at the same time led the Chinese to assimilate the Chinese legal system to that of the West, thereby bringing closer the prospect of the renunciation of extra-territoriality and consular jurisdiction, once this assimilation had been completed. By repealing all the laws enacted by the previous Nationalist government, the Communist government proclaimed its intention of doing away with the Western law introduced in the last few decades. They consciously insisted on foreigners in China submitting themselves to traditional Chinese legal

K

forms, going considerably further by this demand than the government of the traditional China, which had permitted barbarians to live in China according to their own laws (cf. Ch. III, §4 above). That the customary Chinese legal forms were in many respects close to those of other Communist countries makes their adoption even easier to understand. Over and above this, the Communist government endeavoured from the start to deprive foreigners of all the rights which the Chinese government had reluctantly to concede to the Western Powers in the 19th century under the threat of force, such as the right to travel in the country. After 1949 no foreigner, not even a subject of one of the People's Democracies, was allowed to leave the place at which he was living without permission, in order to travel somewhere else. And this permission was by no means granted in every case.

The Christian missionaries had to pay a particularly heavy price for the mistakes of their predecessors, and reaped the hatred that had been sown in the past. It was often not regarded as sufficient to confiscate the movable and immovable property of the missions and expel the foreign missionaries from the country—frequently after a greater or lesser period under arrest. In addition, the attempt was often made, by public discrimination of the grossest description, to deprive individual missionaries of all personal dignity before the mass of the people and to make them contemptible. Sometimes there was a conscious link with events of the 19th century. For example, very severe measures were deliberately taken against the numerous Catholic orphanages, and the old stories were raked up that the foreigners poked out the eyes of the children to make medicine, as well as other tales of atrocities, in order to incite the mob against the missions (cf. Ch. V, §3 above). Everywhere, both at that period and at the present time, the Westerner has been made to feel the weight of Chinese authority and has been forced to realise that he is at most a guest who is temporarily tolerated, but possesses no rights in China. Of course it must not be thought that since 1949 every Chinese has taken part enthusiastically and actively in excesses against individual foreigners; many would have condemned them, and only taken part under pressure. At the same time, there were probably very few Chinese who were entirely free from a feeling of satisfaction, however slight or perhaps even unconscious it may have been, at the way the Westerners had been put in their place.

The numerous technical and military advisers sent to China from the states of the Eastern bloc since 1949, and the members of sundry delegations, are always only temporarily in China for certain specific tasks. They mostly live on their own in special groups of buildings provided for the purpose, and have little contact with the Chinese population. They are strictly controlled, and the Chinese authorities can bring about their recall at any time. They cannot be compared with the Europeans and Americans living in China in the past on their own initiative, and live in an isolation not unlike that of the foreigners before the Opium War.

Thus the events of 1949 signify the end of the era of relations between China and the West which began with the Opium War, the characteristic element of which was Western hegemony in China. The largely emotional attitude that still exists on both sides is due to the after-effects of this era.

VII

China and the West in the 19th and 20th Centuries

1. THE GENERAL CONCEPT OF CHINA IN THE WEST

THE open-minded attitude to China in the West in the 17th and early 18th centuries was increasingly replaced after the end of the 18th century, as we have already described (cf. Ch. IV, §5 above) by an outlook exclusively concentrated upon Europe. An educated European in the 19th century knew far less about China than his predecessors in the 17th and 18th centuries, and he had no interest in this other world, laying as it did outside Western civilisation. People in Europe were proud and self-satisfied at their economic and technical progress, which was in fact unique, and full of contempt for the apparent hopeless backwardness and poverty into which China seemed to have sunk. It was not considered that a mere century previously the greater part of the West had probably been even poorer and more backward.

In the intellectual sphere, an attempt was made to trace the conditions on which the unique contemporary development was based, back into the past history of Europe's own civilisation, based on Greek and Roman antiquity and on Christianity. Europe and its peoples seemed to be the only true bearers of civilisation, to whom no other nation on earth could compare. Only ideas and institutions developed in the West seemed worthy of investigation; everything else was regarded as on a false track and incapable of cultural progress. This basic outlook explains, for example, the statements, which seem most naïve at the present day, made by Hegel and other leading intellectual figures of the 19th century about China, which had a decisive influence on the views held in their time. Thus Hegel, correctly understanding the basic facts, but lacking any detailed knowledge of a development which differed from that of the West, passed the following contemptuous judgement:

> The deficiency of the whole principle of Chinese law lies in its failure to distinguish the sphere of morality from that of law. A reasonable view must recognise that law and morality each belong to their own proper sphere. It is an oriental peculiarity to regard the two principles as one and the same. This peculiarity is found at a stage of moral development, and at a stage in the development of the state, in which morality is still the dominant force. In such a state there is still much which the law fails to provide for, while at the same time it sometimes invades the sphere of morality.[1]

In the same way as Hegel rejected the conjunction of the moral and legal principle by the Chinese, they regarded the separation of the two principles in the West as incomprehensible and barbaric. Even today, this dualism on the part of the West is still strongly condemned in China.

The only source for the knowledge of Chinese history in the 19th century was the lengthy work published from 1777 to 1783 by the Jesuit father De Mailla, *Histoire générale de la Chine*. It is a free redaction of a Chinese work of the 12th century, together with its supplements. This work, *T'ung chien kang-mu*, was in fact not an historical work in the proper sense, but an evaluation of historical events on the basis of the Confucian doctrine of the state. It was bound to give the impression that since the last millenium B.C. up to the present day, everything in China had remained essentially the same. The reader can find in it no trace of a living historical development. Hegel and other Western scholars were satisfied with this superficial impression of China's past, as it seemed to confirm their idea that Western civilisation, having already passed through more phases in its development, was superior. They saw no reason to adopt a critical attitude to their one source, and the thought did not occur to them that China might in reality be able to look back upon an historical development no less varied than that of the West. Thus Hegel wrote that:

[1] Hegel, *Philosophie der Weltgeschichte*, edited by G. Lasson, 2nd ed. II, p. 300.

> The history of China has shown no development, so that we cannot concern ourselves with it any further.[1]

Or:

> We are faced with the oldest state in existence, and yet with one which has no past, but exists at the present time in exactly the same way as we hear of it from antiquity.[2]

Or:

> To this extent, China has no real history.[3]
> China and India lie as it were outside the course of world history.[4]

Ranke's statement is even clearer:

> The British rule the whole world with their trade; they have opened East India and China to Europe, and all these empires are almost submitting to the European spirit.[5]

Elsewhere, Ranke speaks of the Chinese as belonging to the 'nations of eternal stagnation'.[6] If such leading intellectual figures could not look beyond the limits of the European world, how much less capable of this were lesser minds! This example shows clearly how even a creative and independent scholar is always limited in his undersanding by the spatial and temporal conditions of his environment.

The effect of the opinions we have just described lasted far into the 20th century, and even today many European historians cling to the opinion that only the history of Western development is history in the proper sense.

On the other hand, since the end of the first World War more and more voices have been raised in academic circles demanding that the outlook of the 19th century, exclusively

---

[1] ibid. II, p. 283.   [2] ibid. II, p. 278.   [3] ibid. II, p. 278.   [4] ibid. II, p. 275.
[5] *Epochen der neueren Geschichte*, p. 200. Quoted from O. Franke, *Geschichte des Chinesischen Reiches* I, Berlin-Leipzig 1930, p. XI.
[6] *Weltgeschichte*, Part I, 1, pp. VII f. Quoted from O. Franke, ibid. pp. VIf.

orientated towards Europe, be set aside. Thus, for example, Karl Jaspers decisively rejected the views of Hegel and Ranke,

> The automatic assumption that world history consists of a closed circle of Western civilisation has been broken. We can no longer ignore the immense worlds of Asia as nations of eternal stagnation with no history. The scope of world history is universal. Our picture of mankind is incomplete and unbalanced if this scope is restricted.[1]

In line with the disdain with which the academic world treated China, popular literature and the press took China and its population even less seriously in the 19th and 20th centuries. The Chinese were either characterised as uncivilised, inferior and decadent, or else they were represented as comic figures, who could be used in all kinds of ways as an object of mockery and amusement. Everything Chinese was distorted into something absurd and bizarre. This tendency has been maintained right up to the present day, and many journalists and reporters still consider that their readers are better entertained if they describe Chinese affairs with an undertone of the exotic and absurd, instead of trying to give a serious description of reality. And everyone has seen those yellow figures with wide conical hats, long black moustaches and a long pigtail hanging down their backs, which even today, as a relic of the *chinoiserie* of the past, sometimes adorn advertisements for tea and other products, or the dust-covers of books. Even today, large numbers of people in Europe probably still have at least an unconscious conception of the yellow-faced Chinaman with a long pigtail. The pigtail, of course, is not even a Chinese invention, but was a way of wearing the hair imposed upon the Chinese by their Manchu conquerors from the middle of the 17th century up to the end of the Manchu rule in 1911. It would be almost as justifiable to represent Europeans with a pigtail; for did not all men in Europe wear their hair tied behind their head in the 17th and 18th centuries?

On the whole, in the 19th and the early 20th centuries, the

---

[1] K. Jaspers, *Vom Ursprung und Ziel der Geschichte*, Munich 1950, p. 94.

West was considerably less ready to understand China than China was to understand the West. Sustained by the rule of the white man in every part of the earth, which was guaranteed by his better guns, the West usually saw no reason to give serious attention to the peoples of Asia, who were regarded as no more than the objects of colonial exploitation.

2.   THE STUDY OF CHINA IN THE WEST

As we have already mentioned (Ch. VI, §1 above) there was no lack in the West, especially in the second half of the 19th century, of trustworthy accounts of China. Many open-minded Europeans and Americans—missionaries, consular and diplomatic officials, officials of the Imperial Maritime Customs, etc.—were seriously concerned to obtain a more profound understanding of their Chinese environment and its civilisation, although they were not always able to shake off their Western feeling of superiority. Works such as Wells Williams' descriptive study *The Middle Kingdom* (2 vols. 1848), James Legge's translations of a large part of the Canonical Writings of Confucianism, *The Chinese Classics* (8 Vols. 1861–1885), or Baron von Richthofen's great account of his journeys of geographical exploration, *China. Ergebnisse eigener Reisen und darauf gegründete Studien* (1877–1911), are only a few of the most important scientific treaties on China from the 19th century, which are still of value today. Nevertheless, their authors were exceptions to the rule, the effect of their writing was limited, and their influence on scientific study as a whole, as upon the wider public, remained slight. In the atmosphere of the 19th century described above, orientated as it was exclusively towards Europe, there could be no place for the civilisation of China or any other Asian civilisation as an independent branch of study in European scholarship and in the academic institutions of Europe. France, where the universalist tradition of the early 18th century had been of longer duration, provided an exception to this rule within a limited framework. As early as 1818, at France's highest academic institution, the Collège de France, a chair of *Langues et littératures chinoises et tartares manchoues* was founded, which is still in existence. It is significant that this foundation was exclusively for the study of language and literature; no account was taken of other fields such as law, history, art, etc. Thus the academic discipline which was concerned with China received the name 'sinology', and until very recently sinology was largely equated with Chinese philology. Other aspects of Chinese civilisation did not seem worthy of consideration. While the study of other oriental cultures underwent a rapid development in European universities in the 19th century, up to recent years only the very slightest attention has been paid to China in Western academic circles. This is explained by the fact that due to the exclusive orientation towards Europe of Western academic study, oriental civilisations were studied in the first instance purely on the basis of their importance for the civilisations of the West, and especially for Graeco-Roman civilisation. Thus the Near East and Egypt were included from an early period, owing to their links with the Greek world. In the same way, a place was found for the study of India by way of Indo-European philology. For Sanscrit, the classical literary language of India, is in fact an Indo-European language. Unfortunately, the study of China was unable to point to such cultural or linguistic relationships, and consequently the civilisations of East Asia were for a long time regarded as unworthy of consideration. That they ultimately found acceptance was mainly due to three factors. Characteristically, none of these factors was based on a desire to understand the civilisation of Eastern Asia and the forces underlying it; they consisted of:

1.   An exclusively linguistic interest, with no concern for the civilisation underlying the language.

2.   Certain historical connections by way of Central Asia between China and the West through the Turks, Mongols and other non-Chinese peoples.

3.   Practical needs called into being by colonial expansion. Research began to develop, largely following these directions, the main concern being for linguistic studies. The climax of

these studies was reached in 1881 by the publication of the great *Chinesische Grammatik*, an extensive work of over 600 pages, by the linguist and grammarian Georg von der Gabelentz. Here again, to use perhaps a slightly exaggerated expression, the 'intellectual imperialism' of the European was displayed. Gabelentz did not analyse the Chinese language according to any inherent laws of its own, but sought to force it into the categories of Latin grammar, naturally without success. The same occurred in all other branches of study. Every manifestation of Chinese civilisation was measured and judged by standards drawn exclusively from Western developments, but assumed to be absolute. Not only Chinese, but also numerous other languages, living and dead, of the cultural world of Central and Eastern Asia, were studied for their own sake by European scholars. But here we come to the second factor.

European scholars followed the traces of every people who had ever played any part in Western history, or had even merely been mentioned by Greek and Roman authors. Often these traces led towards China, towards the borders of China, in the case not only of the Turks and Mongols, but also of numerous other less important peoples. Many of them had left behind neither their language nor any writing, nor any other records of their civilisation. Thus many scholars learnt Chinese merely in order to be able to make use of Chinese sources historically. And even the sinologists themselves often directed their attention to such small nations on the periphery of China, rather than upon China proper, its civilisation and its history. Thus up to the beginning of the present century, sinology was relatively better informed about numerous non-Chinese peoples on Chinese territory than about the development of Chinese civilisation as such. To give a comparison, it was as though scholars from some non-European country, where little or nothing was known about European civilisation, learned several principal European languages, not in order to use them to learn something about German, English, or French culture—which they completely ignored—but merely in order to go thoroughly into the history of the Basques or the Sorbs for some reason of their own. While the academic world was particularly interested in China from the two points of view already described, an additional factor was the colonial interest of the West, and in connection with this, the needs of the Christian missions. This approach was first adopted in England and France, and later also in Germany. It was concentrated on the one hand on the general knowledge of the country, on the contemporary language, and on modern history, especially that of relations between China and the West. In addition, the missions sought to probe more deeply into the basic religious ideas of China.

These were the prevailing tendencies in sinological research well into the 20th century, and they are still occasionally noticeable at the present day. But in the last 50 years, and especially since the second World War, the main area of study changed more and more. It was increasingly recognised how enormously important the past history of China is for the development of mankind as a whole, and how inadequate our knowledge of it was, and to a large degree still is at the present day. The purely linguistic approach to Chinese studies gave way to a wider concern with what the language expressed. Instead of conducting research from a point of view exclusively oriented towards Europe, into long vanished peripheral peoples and civilisations which were of relatively slight significance for China, the interest of scholars was increasingly applied to the central problems of the development of the Chinese state, its society and its civilisation. And as Western colonialism was increasingly overcome, China was no longer regarded merely as the object of colonial ambition, but an attempt was made to understand how the conflict with the West looked from the Chinese side. Thus since the second World War, the leading role in Chinese studies had passed to the United States, and the readiness of academic circles to include China in their field of study is greater there, in spite of all the widespread prejudices that exist towards China, than in Europe. It is also obvious that geographical conditions, which in the Far West direct attention across the sea to East Asia, as in the East to Europe, are partly responsible for this increasingly open-minded attitude.

The spread of knowledge about the traditional China through the translation of Chinese works led after the first World War, especially in Germany, to a kind of renewal, within a limited framework, of the enthusiasm for China of the 17th and early 18th centuries (cf. Ch. IV, §5 above). Of course it was no longer the unimpressive China of the present day which excited this admiration. These idealistic conceptions were associated much more with the traditional China of the distant past. They took up the profound teachings of Chinese antiquity, such as for example the book *Tao Te Ching*—the *Book of Meaning and Life*, as one German translation entitles it — composed by the legendary personality Lao-tzu, often translated into Western languages, and on the basis of these translations assimilated and as it were re-experienced; or the mysterious *Book of Changes*, about the meaning of which there are many different opinions even in China; or the great Confucius, who bequeathed such fundamental wisdom in his *Analects*. Just as in the 17th and early 18th centuries, such idealisations once again represent in modern times a flight from the reality of a present that often appears hopeless into the unreality of a distant, inaccessible, long dead world. How much more pleasant it is, after all the cares and frustrations of everyday life, to read or to hear how beautiful, how harmonious and how perfect everything once was in China, than to apply one's mind to the serious realities of the bleak and rather unedifying China of the present day! The desire to appease in China's past a longing for a better world, and the contemptuous disdain and lack of interest in China shown by the West, both have this in common, that they hinder an open-minded understanding of present-day realities.

3. CHINA AND THE WEST AT THE PRESENT DAY

The arrogant and superior attitude of the West towards China has increasingly given way in the last ten years to one of fear and hatred. The prevailing idea is expressed in the cliché of a Communist and therefore fundamentally evil and unacceptable 'Red China'. In West Germany in particular the conditions prevailing in East Germany and the feelings people have towards the East German régime are sometimes transferred to China. This highly emotional attitude, which has to be understood in the light of their own involvement due to the partition of Germany herself, complicates any attempt to attain an unprejudiced understanding of present-day China. The hostile attitude of large sections of the American public to China is based on emotion to an even greater degree.

China at the present day is probably even less ready to attempt an objective understanding of the West. In Marxist-Leninist doctrine the 'capitalist-imperialist' countries of the West are regarded simply as representatives of evil. The Western hegemony of the past has left on the Chinese side a considerable legacy of resentment, which official propaganda has not yet wearied of stirring up again and again (Ch. VI, §6 above). Not only do the Chinese still have a lively recollection of the humiliations of the past century, but China's previous status as a universal ruler has also persisted in the consciousness of the Chinese as her normal role (Ch. III, §2, V, §1 above). The Chinese only tolerated the humiliating position into which they had been placed by the West with reluctance and distaste, and always regarded it as transitory and contrary to nature. That China should once again be the first Power in Asia, and should already be able to claim the right to intervene in matters outside Asia, evokes the pride of all Chinese—including to a considerable degree those who at the moment do not live in China itself, and in other respects are opposed to the Peking government. But the representatives of this government consider themselves the heirs of 2,000 years of imperial tradition, and are even seeking to win back for China the status in her frontier regions which she possessed before the Western and Japanese expansion in the 19th century.

The renewed tradition of China as a world Power in the full sense means that the slight offered to her by the refusal of other nations to recognise her, and admit her to the United Nations, is felt as a particularly bitter insult. China's disgust at this has led to an increasingly strained attitude to the West, although here again—as so often in the past—rhetorical and aggressive language has gone hand in hand with caution and discretion in political action. By increased initiatives in the countries of Asia, Africa and even South America, the attempt has been made to build up China's new status as a world Power, in conscious opposition to the policy of the West. The numerous delegations which come in admiration from these countries to China are the successors of the tribute embassies of earlier periods (Ch. III, §2 above).[1] Just as in the past, they contribute to the political prestige of the Chinese government. By the magnificent reception and careful attention accorded to them, the splendour and power of China are visibly demonstrated, and rarely fail to make their impression on envoys from less sophisticated and less developed countries. In addition, an appeal is made to their emotions against the previous or even present rule of the Western Powers in the country from which the guests come, and they are shown how China has freed herself from the century-long hegemony of the West, and brought her power to a hitherto unknown level. It is implied that if their countries rely on the example and leadership of China, they can be assured of similar progress.

In view of this challenge, the West cannot afford to persist in an attitude which is no more than a cliché, and which prevents any thorough understanding of China. The attitude of China to the West in the 19th century should serve as a warning. It is true that in many respects the situation is fundamentally different nowadays, but the lack of a willingness to abandon a way of thought exclusively centred upon

---

[1] In the historical accounts at the present day the tribute embassies of the past are sometimes referred to by the modern term 'delegation' (*tai-piao t'uan*).

one's own world and standards, and to recognise without prejudice what lies behind those of the other side, is the same in both cases. China did not seek communication with the Western world on her own initiative, but was forced into an encounter with her. Today it is the West that is faced with a challenge to accept an encounter with the new China and her initiatives in the rest of the world, without there being any need for the West to undergo such painful experiences as China had to suffer in the 19th and early 20th centuries. The first requirement in this is the most thorough knowledge possible of present-day China, and a willingness to understand without prejudice the forces that guide the development of China. Such a willingness on the part of men in the West is the only possible basis for a response to this challenge. The encounter may then perhaps lead to the synthesis between China and the West for which Leibniz was groping in a vague form, and without which no peace is conceivable in the world.

Chronology of the Chinese Dynasties and Important Dates in the Relations between China and the West

Before the 12th or 11th century B.C. Shang-Yin Dynasty

12th or 11th century B.C.-255 B.C. Chou Dynasty

722–481 B.C.   Period of *The Spring and Autumn Annals*

481–221 B.C.   Period of the Warring States

221–207 B.C.   Ch'in Dynasty

202 B.C.–
221 A.D.   Han Dynasty

138–126 B.C.   Embassy of Chang Ch'ien to Western Central Asia

97 A.D.   Chinese travellers reach the Persian Gulf by way of Central Asia

1st and 2nd
centuries A.D.   Greek authors mention Seres and Sinae

221–264 A.D.   Period of the Three Kingdoms

265–420   Chin Dynasty

420–589   Period of the separation between North and South China

589–618   Sui Dynasty

618–906   T'ang Dynasty

Ca. 630   Theophylactos of Simocatta describes Taugast

907–960   Period of the Five Dynasties

960–1279   Sung Dynasty

937–1125   Liao Dynasty (Kitan) in the North

1115–1234   Chin Dynasty (Juchen) in the North

1245–1247   Journey of Piano Carpini to Mongolia

1253–1255   Journey of William of Rubruk to Mongolia

1279–1367   Yüan Dynasty (Mongol)

1275–1292   Marco Polo in Mongolia and China

1330   Chinese map of the world, showing Europe and Africa

1368–1644   Ming Dynasty

1403–1433   Chinese maritime expeditions reached the Red Sea and the Persian Gulf

1509	The Portuguese in Malacca
1513 (1514)	The Portuguese in China
1582–1610	Matteo Ricci in China
1601	The Dutch in China
1602–1605	The journey of Benedict de Goëz demonstrates the identity of Kitai and China (Sina)
1625	The British in China
1644–1911	Ch'ing Dynasty (Manchu)
1645–1661	Adam Schall von Bell a Chinese official
1662	First translation into Latin of part of the Confucian Canon
1697	Publication of Leibniz's *Novissima Sinica*
1721	Christian Wolff's university lecture *De Sinarum philosophia practica*
1814	The establishment of a chair of Chinese language and literature at the *Collège de France*
1840–1842	Opium War between China and Britain
1854	The establishment of the Chinese Imperial Maritime Customs under foreign administration
1858	The treaties of Tientsin
1860	British and French troops advance to Peking
1861	The Tsungli-Yamen set up to deal with foreign affairs
1870	Outbreaks of violence against the Christian missions in Tientsin, known as the 'Tientsin Massacre'
1876	The first permanent Chinese diplomatic representation abroad
1885	France occupies Annam
1886	Britain occupies Burma
1894–1895	War between China and Japan
1897	Germany occupies the Kiaochou region
1898	Russia occupies Dairen and Port Arthur, France occupies Kuangchouwan, and Britain occupies Weihaiwei— Climax of Chinese reform movement
1900	'Boxer Rising' against the foreigners in Peking and North China
1905	Abolition of the traditional official examination system

1911–12	Revolution and abdication of the last dynasty
1912–1949	The Republic
1919	The 'May Fourth Movement'
1925–1927	The Anti-imperialist movement
1937–1945	War between China and Japan
1943	The formal ending of the 'unequal treaties' between China and the Western powers
1946	The Catholic Church of China becomes an independent branch of the Catholic hierarchy
1949	The People's Republic of China
1949	The expulsion of most Westerners by the new Chinese government

Selected Bibliography

In the following bibliography only a very limited selection of titles are given, which may help the interested reader to study the subject more deeply. Only books in Western languages are given. The following abbreviations are used for the titles of journals:

HJAS   Harvard Journal of Asiatic Studies, Cambridge, Mass.
MS   Monumenta Serica, Peking and Nagoya.
TP   T'oung Pao, Leiden.

Ch. 1
1   Yule-Cordier, *Cathay and the Way Thither*, 2nd ed. London, 1915, Vol. 1.
2   F. Hirth, *China and the Roman Orient*, Shanghai, 1885.
3   Geoffrey F. Hudson, *Europe and China: A Survey of Their Relations from the Earliest Times to 1800*, London, 1931, Reprint Boston 1961.
4   Otto Franke, *Geschichte des Chinesischen Reiches*, Berlin-Leipzig, Vol. 1, 1930; Vol. III, 1936.
5   Peter A. Boodberg, 'Marginalia to the Histories of the Northern Dynasties, I. Theophylactus Simocatta on China', *HJAS* 3, 1938, pp. 223–243.
6   Joseph Needham, *Science and Civilisation in China*, Vol. 1, Cambridge, 1954.

Ch. 2. General
7   A. C. Moule, *Christians in China before the Year 1550*, London, 1930.
    Also No. 1, Vol. 1 and Vol. 3; No. 3; No. 4, Vol. IV, 1948.

Ch. 2. 1
8   Friedrich Risch, *Johann de Piano Carpini. Geschichte der Mongolen und Reisebericht 1245–1247*, Leipzig, 1930.

Ch. 2. 2
9   Friedrich Risch, *Wilhelm von Rubruk. Reise zu den Mongolen 1253–1255*, Leipzig, 1934.

Ch. 2. 3
10 Yule-Cordier, *The Book of Ser Marco Polo*, 3rd ed., 2 vols., London, 1903.

11 Benedetto, *Marco Polo, il milione*, Florence, 1928. Engl. translation by Aldo Ricci, *The Travels of Marco Polo*, London, 1931.

12 Moule-Pelliot, *Marco Polo, The Description of the World*, 2 vols., London, 1938.

13 H. Cordier, *Les voyages en Asie au XIV siècle du bienheureux frère Odorico de Pordenone*, Paris, 1891.

14 A. C. Moule in *TP* 20, 1921, pp. 275–290, 301–322; 21, 1922, pp. 387–393. (Various observations on Odorico de Pordenone.)

Ch. 2. 5

15 E. Bretschneider, *Mediaeval Researches from Eastern Asiatic Sources*, 2 vols., London, 1888.

16 Walter Fuchs, *The 'Mongol Atlas' of China*, Peking, 1946.

Ch. 3. General

17 John K. Fairbank—Edwin O. Reischauer—Albert M. Craig, *East Asia. The Modern Transformation*, Boston, 1965.

18 H. Cordier, 'L'arrivée des Portugais en Chine' *TP* 12, 1911, pp. 482–543.

19 Chang T'ien-tse, *Sino-Portuguese Trade from 1514 to 1644*, Leiden, 1934. Reviewed by P. Pelliott in *TP* 31, 1935, pp. 58–94.

20 J. M. Braga, *The Western Pioneers and Their Discovery of Macao*, Macao, 1949.

21 Albert Kammerer, *La découverte de la Chine par les Portugais au XVIème siècle et la cartographie des Portulans*, Leiden, 1944. Also No. 3.

Ch. 3. 1

22 P. Pelliot, 'Les grands voyages maritimes Chinois au début du XVe sièle', *TP* 30, 1933, pp. 237–452; 31, 1935, pp. 274–314; 32, 1936, pp. 210–222.

23 J. J. L. Duyvendak, *Ma Huan Re-examined*, Amsterdam, 1933.

24 J. J. L. Duyvendak, 'The True Dates of the Chinese Maritime Expeditions in the Early Fifteenth Century', *TP* 34, 1939, pp. 341–412.

25 J. J. L. Duyvendak, *China's Discovery of Africa*, London, 1949.

Ch. 3. 2

26 Owen Lattimore, *Inner Asian Frontiers of China*, New York, 1940 and 1951.

27 J. K. Fairbank—S. Y. Teng, 'On the Ch'ing Tributary System', *HJAS* 6, 1941, pp. 135–246.

28 J. K. Fairbank, *Trade and Diplomacy on the China Coast. The Opening of the Treaty Ports 1842 to 1854*, 2 vols., Cambridge, Mass., 1953.

29 J. K. Pannikar, *Asia and Western Dominance*, London, 1953.

Ch. 3. 3
30 P. Pelliot, 'Le Ḫoja et le Sayyid Husain de l'histoire des Ming', *TP* 38, 1948, pp. 81–282.

Ch. 3. 4
31 C. R. Boxer, *Fidalgoes in the Far East, 1550–1770. Fact and Fancies in the History of Macao*, The Hague, 1948.
32 Søren Egerod, 'A note on the Origin of the Name of Macao', *TP* 47, 1959, pp. 63–66.

Ch. 4 General
33 Louis Pfister, *Notices biographiques et bibliographiques sur les Jésuites de l'ancienne mission de Chine 1552–1773*, 2 vols., Shanghai, 1932–34.
34 Pasquale M. d'Elia, *The Catholic Missions in China*, Shanghai, 1934.
35 Pasquale M. d'Elia, *Fonti Ricciane*. vol. I–III: *Storia dell' introduzione del cristianesimo in Cina scritta da Matteo Ricci S.J.*, Rome, 1942–49.
36 Louis J. Gallagher, *China in the Sixteenth Century*: *The Journals of Matthew Ricci 1583–1610*, Toronto, 1953.
37 Henri Bernard, *Matteo Ricci's Scientific Contributions to China*, Peking, 1935.
38 Henri Bernard, *Le père Matthieu Ricci et la société Chinoise de son temps (1552–1610)*, 2 vols., Tientsin, 1937.
39 Kenneth Scott Latourette, *A History of Christian Missions in China*, New York, 1929.
40 Otto Franke, *Li Tschi und Matteo Ricci. Abhandlungen der Preußischen Akademie der Wissenschaften* (1938) No. 5, Berlin, 1939.
41 George H. Dunne, *Generation of Giants. The Story of the Jesuits in China in the last Decades of the Ming Dynasty*, London, 1962.

Ch. 4. 1
42 C. R. Boxer, *South China in the Sixteenth Century, Being the narratives of Galeote Pereira, Fr. Gaspar da Cruz, O.P., Fr. Martin de Rada, O.R.D.S. (1550–1575)*, London, 1953.

Ch. 4. 2
43 Robert Chabrié, *Michel Boym, Jésuite Polonais et la fin des Ming en Chine (1642–1662)*, Paris, 1933. Reviewed by P. Pelliot in *TP* 31, 1935, pp. 95–151.

44 Fr. Jäger, 'Dokumente über Kü Schï-sï', *Sinica-Sonderausgabe* 1934, pp. 11–22.
45 Arthur W. Hummel (ed.), *Eminent Chinese of the Ch'ing Period (1644–1912)*, 2 vols., Washington, D.C., 1943–44.
46 C. W. Allan, *Jesuits at the Court of Peking*, Shanghai, (no date).

Ch. 4. 3
47 Alfons Väth, *Johann Adam Schall von Bell S.J.*, Cologne, 1933.
48 Pasquale M. d'Elia, *Galileo in China. Relations through the Roman College between Galileo and the Jesuit Scientist-Missionaries (1610–1640)*, Cambridge, Mass., 1960.
49 Joseph Needham, *Chinese Astronomy and the Jesuit Mission*, London, 1958.
     Also No. 39., 41.

Ch. 4. 4
50 Malcolm Hay, *Failure in the Far East. Why and How the Breach between the Western World and China first began*, Wetteren, Belgium, 1956.
     Also No. 39, 41, 44, 45.

Ch. 4. 5
51 Virgile Pinot, *La Chine et la formation de l'esprit philosophique en France (1640–1740)*, Paris, 1932.
52 Virgile Pinot, *Documents inédits relatifs à la connaissance de la Chine en France de 1685–1740*, Paris, 1932.
53 Edgar Schorer, *L'influence de la Chine sur la genèse et le development de la doctrine physiocratique*, Paris, 1938.
54 Adolf Reichwein, *China and Europe; intellectual and artistic contacts in the eighteenth century*, New York—London, 1925.
55 Donald Lach, *The Preface to Leibniz' Novissima Sinica*, Honolulu, 1958.
56 William W. Appleton, *A Cycle of Cathay*, New York, 1951.
57 Lewis A. Maverick, *China, A Model for Europe*, San Antonio, 1946.

Ch. 5. General
58 Henri Cordier, *Histoire des relations de la Chine avec les puissances occidentales 1860–1902*, 3 vols., Paris, 1901–02.
59 H. B. Morse, *The International Relations of the Chinese Empire*, 3 vols., Shanghai, 1910–18.
60 *Treaties, Conventions, etc. between China and Foreign States*, Ed. China. The Maritime Customs, 2 vols., 2nd ed. Shanghai, 1917.

61 Arthur Waley, *The Opium War Through Chinese Eyes*, London, 1958.
62 Hsin-pao Chang, *Commissioner Liu and the Opium War*, Cambridge, Mass., 1964.
63 Westel W. Willoughby, *Foreign Rights and Interests in China*, 2 vols., Baltimore, 1927.
64 S. F. Wright, *Hart and the Chinese Customs*, Belfast, 1950.
65 S. F. Wright, *China's Struggle for Tariff Autonomy: 1843–1938*, Shanghai, 1938.
66 Masataka Banno, *China and the West 1858–1861*, Cambridge, Mass., 1964.
67 Immanuel C. Y. Hsü, *China's Entrance into the Family of Nations. The Diplomatic Phase 1858–1880*, Cambridge, Mass., 1960.
68 John K. Fairbank, *The United States and China*, Cambridge, Mass., 1958.
   Also No. 28, 45.

Ch. 5. 3
69 Paul A. Cohen, *China and Christianity. The Missionary Movement and the Growth of Chinese Antiforeignism, 1860–1870*, Cambridge, Mass., 1963.
70 Wolfgang Franke, 'Zur anti-imperialistischen Bewegung in China', *Saeculum* 5, 1954, pp. 337–358.
   Also No. 39.

Ch. 5. 4
71 Mary C. Wright, *The Last Stand of Chinese Conservatism. The T'ungchih Restoration, 1862–1874*, Stanford, Calif., 1957.
72 Nathan A. Pelcovits, *Old China Hands and the Foreign Office*, New York, 1948.
73 A. H. Exner, *China*, Leipzig, 1889.
   Also No. 68, 70.

Ch. 6 General
74 Ssu-yü Teng—John K. Fairbank, *China's Response to the West, a documentary survey 1839–1923*, Cambridge, Mass., 1954.
75 Wolfgang Franke, *Das Jahrhundert der chinesischen Revolution, 1815–1949*, Munich, 1958.
76 Joseph R. Levenson, *Confucian China and its Modern Fate*, 3 vols., Berkeley, Calif., 1958–1965.
77 E. R. Hughes, *The Invasion of China by the Western World*, New York, 1938.
   Also No. 68.

Ch. 6. 1
78 Tsuen-hsuin Tsien, 'Western Impact on China through Trans-
    lation', *Far Eastern Quarterly*, 13, 1954, pp. 305–327.
    Also No. 28, 45, 61, 67, 71.

Ch. 6. 2
79 M. E. Cameron, *The Reform Movement in China 1898–1912*,
    Stanford, Calif., 1931.
80 Kung-ch'üan Hsiao, 'K'ang Yu-wei and Confucianism', *MS*
    18, 1959, pp. 96–212.
81 Kung-ch'üan Hsiao, 'The philosophical thought of K'ang
    Yu-wei; an attempt at a new synthesis', *MS* 21, 1962, pp. 129–
    193.
82 Benjamin Schwartz, *In Search of Wealth and Power. Yen Fu and
    the West*, Cambridge, Mass., 1964.
83 Jérome Tobar, *K'iuen-hio P'ien. Exhortations à l'étude par . . .
    Tchang Tsche-tong*, Shanghai, 1909.
    Also No. 45.

Ch. 6. 3
84 Wolfgang Franke, *The Reform and Abolition of the Traditional
    Chinese Examination System*, Cambridge, Mass., 1960.
85 Cyrus H. Peake, *Nationalism and Education in Modern China*,
    New York, 1932.

Ch. 6. 4
86 Wolfgang Franke, *Chinas kulturelle Revolution. Die Bewegung vom
    4. Mai 1919*, Munich, 1957.
87 Chow Tse-tsung, *The May Fourth Movement*, Cambridge, Mass.,
    1960.

Ch. 6. 5 and 6
88 T. and S. Yamamoto, 'The Anti-Christian Movement in China
    1922–27', *Far Eastern Quarterly*, 12/2, 1953, pp. 133–147.
89 Tang Tsou, *America's Failure in China 1941–1950*, Chicago, 1963.
    Also No. 70, 86.

Ch. 7
90 Mary Gertrude Mason, *Western Concepts of China and the Chinese*,
    1840–1876, New York, 1939.
91 Edwin G. Pulleyblank, 'China', in *Orientalism and History*, ed.
    by Denis Sinor, Cambridge, 1954.
92 John K. Fairbank, 'A Note of Ambiguity: Asian Studies in
    America', *Journal of Asian Studies* 19/1, 1959, pp. 3–9.

INDEX

Date Due